ARMS CONTROL AND STRATEGIC STABILITY

Challenges for the Future

Edited by

William T. Parsons

Proceedings from the Third Annual Seminar of the
Center for Law and National Security at
Charlottesville on June 22-24, 1984

UNIVERSITY
PRESS OF
AMERICA

LANHAM • NEW YORK • LONDON

Copyright © 1986 by

University Press of America,® Inc.

4720 Boston Way
Lanham, MD 20706

3 Henrietta Street
London WC2E 8LU England

Library of Congress Cataloging in Publication Data

University of Virginia. Center for Law and National
    Security.   Seminar (3rd : 1984 : Charlottesville,
    Va.)
    Arms control and strategic stability.

    "Proceedings of the third annual Seminar of the Center
for Law and National Security at Charlottesville on
June 22-24, 1984."
    "Co-published by arrangement with the Center for Law
and National Security"—T.p. verso.
    1. Arms control—Congresses.   2. Nuclear arms
control—United States—Congresses.   3. Nuclear arms
control—Soviet Union—Congresses.   4. Strategic
Defense Initiative—Congresses.   I. Parsons, William T.
(William Terrill), 1955-   .   II. University of
Virginia.   Center for Law and National Security.
III. Title.
JX1974.U65   1984   327.1'74   86-13256
    ISBN 0-8191-5474-1 (alk. paper)
    ISBN 0-8191-5475-X (pbk. : alk. paper)

All University Press of America books are produced on acid-free
paper which exceeds the minimum standards set by the National
Historical Publications and Records Commission.

CONTENTS

iii

INTRODUCTION

by

James H. Doyle, Jr.
Vice Admiral, U.S. Navy (retired)
Plans and Programs, Center for
Law and National Security

The Center for Law and National Security was established at the University of Virginia School of Law, Charlottesville, Virginia in 1981. Created as a nonpartisan and nonprofit institution, the Center is dedicated to fostering informed public discussion on the legal and policy aspects of national security issues. One of the Center's most important objectives is to provide avenues for thoughtful debate on nuclear weapons and arms control.

Toward this end, the Center sponsors annual seminars and periodic forum discussions on Capital Hill. In addition, courses are offered at the University of Virginia School of Law in Law and National Security as well as in Nuclear Weapons and Arms Control. Finally, the Center sponsors research and publishes monographs on various issues involving law and national security. The Director of the Center is John Norton Moore, the Water L. Brown Professor of Law at the University of Virginia.

On June 22-24, 1984, at the University of Virginia School of Law in Thomas Jefferson's historic Charlottesville, the Center devoted its third annual seminar to the subject of Arms Control and Strategies Stability. This publication contains the proceedings of that seminar which consisted of two keynote addresses, four formal panel discussions and one informal wrap-up session. As the reader will see, we were fortunate in gathering a distinguished group of statesmen, lawyers, political-military leaders and technical experts from both government and the private sector. These proceedings were edited by William T. Parsons, then a senior fellow at the Center and now with the Office of General Counsel, Arms Control and Disarmament Agency. He also assists in teaching the course in Nuclear Weapons and Arms Control at the University of Virginia.

At the outset, let me emphasize that the title of the seminar was chosen with care. We at the Center firmly believe that there can be no meaningful discussions of arms control without a full exploration of all aspects of strategic stability. This includes discussion of U.S. and Soviet nuclear strategies; the differing concepts of deterrence and warfighting; the intangibles of credibility and perception; the realities of strategic offense and defense and their interrelationships; the operational, technical, schedule and cost implications of various weapons programs; the impact of policies and programs on East-West relations and NATO-Warsaw Pact cohesiveness; the linkage with the conventional weapons balance; and the capabilities of third parties and terrorists. Similarly, meaningful discussions of strategic stability must include exploration of various arms control issues including prior arms control treaties and agreements, linkage with other negotiations, confidence-building and risk-reduction measures, and verification and noncompliance. During this brief seminar, we were only able to explore a few of the key issues, but discussions were conducted within the broad context of arms control *and* strategic stability.

The leadoff keynote speaker was Robert C. McFarlane, then Assistant to the President for National Security Affairs. He provided a comprehensive description of the Reagan Administration's approach to arms control and explained why arms control is and must be an inseparable part of the U.S. overall security and foreign policy. His message was clear: "arms control is a means to achieve U.S. goals of peace, security and freedom; it is not an end in itself."

Dr. George A. Keyworth, II, Science Adviser to the President, in his keynote address explained the Administration's Strategic Defense Initiative, dubbed "Star Wars." He stated why, in his opinion, SDI can be a stabilizing factor that will permit both the U.S. and Soviet Union to reduce their reliance on huge arsenals of nuclear weapons. In Dr. Keyworth's words, SDI "is our attempt to use the tools we have-- modern technology--to rewrite the strategic equations so that we can look forward to a reasonably stable world for generations to come."

The four formal panel discussions, with prepared papers, tackled the issues of the "Impact of Weapon Technology: Space and Beyond," "Start and INF: Search for East-West Stability," "Confidence Building and Risk Reduction Measures," and "Verification and Compliance." The discussions by distinguished experts was informal and lively. Disagreements over both policy and implementation were articulated in a most professional manner, devoid of the usual emotional rhetoric and designed to contribute toward construc- tive solutions. The Administration's arms control policy and strategies defense initiative were both supported and criticized. Audience participation enhanced discussion in all sessions.

The final panel entitled "The Future of Arms Control" was an informal and unrehearsed discussion by panelists who had participated in previous panels. The moderator was John Norton Moore, Director of the Center, who set the stage by posing a series of wide-ranging issues. Discussion centered on the pros and cons of the Reagan Administration's approach to arms control, particularly in the area of U.S./Soviet noncompliance with arguments, technical violations, import of SDI on the ABM Treaty, confidence-build- ing, various aspects of strategic stability, ASAT ban, weapon modernization, East-West relations and "selling" arms control agreements in the Congress. Again, audience participation contributed to focussing the debate.

Feedback on the seminar from panelists and other attendees was positive and encouraging. All com- mented on the professional atmosphere of the debate and discussion. We hope that the proceedings of the seminar will contribute toward a greater understanding of the issues and play some constructive part in solving the complex problems in arms control and strategic stability.

PART I

ARMS CONTROL AND
STRATEGIC STABILITY

CHAPTER 1

EFFECTIVE ARMS CONTROL: CHALLENGE OF THE 1980s

by

The Honorable Robert C. McFarlane
Assistant to the President for National Security
Affairs, National Security Council

The task of preserving America's freedom has never been more important, or complex, than it is today. As never before, our freedom, our prosperity, and our security--and those of our allies in the free world--require that we maintain a stable peace. Notwithstanding the spotty record of history, it is clear that arms control can make a contribution to a more stable peace. If we are to be successful we must persevere. We welcome the help of thoughtful scholars and analysts in that effort.

From my daily contact with President Reagan, there is no question of his deep personal commitment to arms reductions. That commitment is reflected in the scope of his efforts and in the boldness of his initiatives--deep reductions in START, the elimination of an entire category of INF weapons, regular United States-Soviet consultations on nuclear proliferation, the first steps of a new crisis management system in the Hot Line talks--to mention just a few of our initiatives with the Soviet Union designed to reduce danger of a nuclear conflict.

Our multilateral agenda for conventional arms control is ambitious as well. At the Mutual and Balanced Force Reductions (MBFR) talks in Vienna, we have presented with our NATO allies an innovative proposal designed to reduce the size of conventional forces in Europe. At the Stockholm Conference on

Confidence and Security Building Measures and Disarmament (CDE), the West has proposed measures designed to enhance mutual confidence in Europe and to reduce the risk of surprise attack. At the Geneva Conference on Disarmament (CD), we continue to work with 39 other nations on very difficult, but vital, issues including nuclear testing and space arms control as well as a comprehensive ban on chemical weapons. We recognize that achievement of effective arms control is a formidable challenge. If we remain true to our principles and steady in our resolve, however, we shall succeed.

Arms Control and Security

I would like to describe the Reagan Administration's approach to arms control. Also, I will explain why arms control is and must be an inseparable part of our nation's overall security and foreign policy. Arms control cannot be isolated from the complex realities of the world. Instead, we must recognize that it is a dependent variable in our overall national security policy and is a part--but not the whole--of the broader United States-Soviet relationship. Arms control is a means to achieve our goals of peace, security and freedom; it is not an end in itself.

The President has been working hard to strengthen the United States-Soviet dialogue. In a major address on January 16, 1984, he outlined in some detail his objectives for establishing a productive and realistic long-term relationship with the Soviet Union. To last, such a relationship must be based on the principles of realism, restraint and reciprocity. Important as it is, arms control cannot carry the entire United States-Soviet relationship. The Soviet invasion of Afghanistan in 1979 showed that we must take care of other aspects of superpower interaction. Otherwise, our national security, and the arms control process itself, will suffer.

Real arms control in the real world does not admit of simple solutions promoted by simple slogans; nor will effective arms control be achieved by dividing into partisan camps whose boundaries are marked by

4

false dichotomies, harsh rhetoric and extremist views. For example, some believe arms control weakens the security of democracies; for others it is a panacea for the ills of the world. In fact, arms control can either help or hinder, depending on whether or not we do a good job of it. The Reagan Administration's approach to arms control has been guided from the beginning by four interrelated tenets. Real arms control agreements must be equitable, militarily significant, effectively verifiable and stabilizing. In short, they should contribute to the maintenance of a lasting peace.

Our first premise, that arms control agreements must be equitable, should be obvious. The United States does not seek military superiority over the Soviet Union. However, we cannot allow the Soviet Union to have superiority over us. The balance we seek is one in which both sides retain secure, stable nuclear retaliatory forces and neither side is threatened by the military might of the other.

Any settlement with the Soviet Union will involve trade-offs between areas of American advantage and areas of Soviet advantage, but no president can accept an agreement which favors the Soviet Union. Congress would not ratify it and the American people would not accept it. Yet, the Soviet Union will not settle for equitable agreements if we are not able to demonstrate a resolve to maintain the balance. While this does not mean that we must have precise equality to negotiate, the Soviets are not going to give us something for nothing.

We do not build weapons systems or force structures simply as bargaining chips. Our programs are designed to enhance deterrence by maintaining the balance. For example, the MX missile--the Peacekeeper--is a vital part of ensuring that we can respond effectively to a Soviet attack, thus assuring that the war we all agree must never happen, never does. I have yet to hear, from those who oppose the MX, what incentive the Soviets will have to accept real reductions in their own ICBM force if we unilaterally forego our modernization program. In the last few years alone the Soviet Union has deployed some 800 new medium or heavy missiles. Further-

5

more, the Soviet Union already has tested two new strategic missiles and continues to invest heavily to ensure the effectiveness of their missile force. Since SALT I was signed in 1972, the Soviets have introduced 31 new or modified strategic systems and they have vastly increased their nuclear forces since the 1960s. In contrast, between SALT I and SALT II, the United States introduced only one new strategic system, the Short Range Attack Missile (SRAM), and that was to aid our aging bomber force.

Annual Soviet military investment has grown consistently over the last two decades to double our own by the early 1980s. Soviet investment in strategic nuclear forces was about three times our own during 1980-81. This disparity has weakened deterrence around the world and undermined our efforts at the negotiating table. Long-overdue modernization will help redress the military balance and will enhance our ability to negotiate a stable agreement at reduced levels.

We do not build simply to build. In fact, the United States nuclear stockpile is at its lowest level in twenty years. The total number of weapons today was reduced by 25 percent from 1967 levels. In addition, the total megatonnage of our current stockpile is only one quarter of that which we possessed 25 years ago.

The second premise is that arms control agreements should be of military significance. Declarations such as "no-first-use of nuclear weapons" are no substitute for meaningful arms control. That is why, in the Stockholm Conference on Confidence and Security Building Measures and Disarmament (CDE), the United States and its allies have proposed concrete measures which would increase our confidence that the Warsaw Pact is not preparing for offensive action and provide them with comparable assurances. By contrast, the Soviet Union has focused much of its attention on declaratory measures renouncing the use of force, but which contain no tangible improvement in security. Nonetheless, the President made clear in his recent address to the Irish Parliament that we are willing to consider this Soviet proposal if the Soviets and their allies take concrete steps toward the package of measures proposed by the West in Stockholm.

Equally important, arms control agreements which only codify levels of armaments at ever higher plateaus, or which freeze us into an increasingly destabilizing imbalance, do not begin to address the real problems posed by modern weapons. Indeed, they make it more difficult to achieve effective arms control. For this reason, President Reagan has advanced serious proposals that cut deeply into existing United States and Soviet nuclear arsenals. We will continue to pursue our goal of a nuclear balance at significantly lower levels.

Our third tenet is that arms control agreements must be verifiable. When you look at the stark contrast between our open American society and the closed nature of the Soviet system, I am sure you will agree that these agreements, which often go to the heart of our national security, cannot be based on trust. Furthermore, Soviet violations of earlier agreements regarding the use of chemical and biological weapons, the Helsinki Final Act, SALT II, and almost certainly the ABM Treaty, underscore the need for effective verification. Our concerns are further aggravated by examples such as the Threshold Test Ban Treaty, where we consider Soviet violations likely, but cannot obtain conclusive proof because of the lack of effective verification provisions. The Soviet Union has been thus far unwilling to agree even to begin discussions of improved verification of the Threshold Test Ban Treaty and the Treaty on Peaceful Nuclear Explosions. Their willingness to do so will be an important determinant of our willingness to enter even more difficult domains of verification.

What lesson should we draw from Soviet noncompliance and resistance to effective verification provisions? Should we abandon the quest for new agreements? Must we simply accept abuse of the arms control process? No. We must persist in requiring acceptance of effective means of verification, record them in treaties, and insist on compliance with those agreements. If we failed to do this, there would be little confidence left in the entire arms control process.

Perfect verification will never be possible, and not

all agreements will require the same degree of monitoring or cooperative measures, but all will benefit from more careful attention to problem areas such as legal drafting, non-interference with National Technical Means of Verification, active and passive cooperative measures, inspection regimes, and safeguards against violation or breakout. In short, effective verification agreements, procedures and circumstances each require that we as a government be able to make responsible, but prompt, judgments concerning circumventions or violations well before there is a risk to our security.

The fourth basic tenet is that arms control must contribute to strategic and regional stability. Often, we as a nation have focused on limitations without due regard for the implications of those limitations. For example, in both SALT I and SALT II, preoccupation with launcher limits without sufficient limits on the military capabilities of the missiles that would be fired from those launchers has made maintaining a stable nuclear balance more difficult. Indeed, we moved away from our own 850 limit in START in order to avoid the same mistake. Mobile missiles and small single warhead missiles, once viewed as impediments to arms control, are now viewed by a sizeable part of the arms control community as essential to future stability.

If we are to maintain a stable balance into the next century, and if we are to do so at far lower levels of nuclear arms, we must be more creative in our thinking. That is the spirit behind the President's Strategic Defense Initiative (SDI). The President has set in motion a long-term study of policy and technology options aimed at reducing the threat to the United States and our allies posed by increases in Soviet offensive capabilities, thus enhancing stability and eliminating incentives for further growth of offensive armaments. Rather than a near-term, quick fix to vulnerability problems, it represents a long-term vision of a safer world for future generations.

Enhancing strategic stability and reducing American and Soviet weapons stockpiles will not solve our nuclear security concerns if we neglect the problem of the spread of nuclear weapons. Accordingly, the

8

Reagan Administration has taken nuclear nonproliferation seriously, and has worked vigorously but quietly
with others to perfect mechanisms of export control.
While we try to keep technical barriers to proliferation high, we realize that reducing the conditions that
give rise to proliferation must be the central premise
of our nonproliferation policy. Our conventional
security program with Pakistan is fashioned around
this premise. In addition to reducing the incentives
for nuclear proliferation, we have worked to get other
supplier nations to join the United States in insisting
on comprehensive safeguards before supplying nuclear
materials for peaceful purposes.

Unchecked, nuclear proliferation will complicate
other arms control initiatives and severely increase
regional dangers. Reducing the incentives and the
opportunities for proliferation is an exacting task, but
important to achieving the objective of stability. By
reducing the potential for conflict, enhancing stability
in turn contributes to deterrence.

The Role of Deterrence

The importance of deterrence is best seen in
historical perspective. In the first half of the
twentieth century over 100 million people died in
conventional wars. In the forty years since the
nuclear age began, however, there have been no wars
in Europe, a feat unmatched in 400 years of European
history--no world wars and no nuclear wars. On the
other hand, nuclear weapons have not eliminated
aggression or changed the basic causes of war.
Outside Europe, where strong defensive alliances like
NATO have not existed, some 130 military conflicts
have taken place since 1945. Nor have nuclear
weapons prevented the Soviet Union from relentlessly
increasing its military might, or from seeking to
expand its influence by armed force and threats.

For 35 years, the NATO alliance has stood firm
against Soviet advances in Western Europe. But
Soviet interventionism in the Third World demon-
strates that wherever weaknesses exist, the Soviets
will attempt to exploit them. We cannot allow this

behavior to go unopposed. The burdens which this places on the United States are considerable. If we wish to preserve peace and freedom, we must be willing to build the forces necessary to achieve that goal. We must have the political will to join our friends and allies in resisting aggression, subversion, terrorism and intimidation. Toward that end we must continue to maintain a balanced deterrent of both nuclear and conventional forces, and we look to arms control to aid us in that process.

The Soviet military buildup of the 1970s was particularly threatening in the area of nuclear weapons. Not content to attain nuclear parity, the Soviets expanded their capabilities to the point of achieving important advantages in several areas. Substantial quantitative and qualitative increases in Soviet strategic weapons are posing a fundamental challenge to the deterrence which has kept the peace since 1945. The Soviets also took advantage of gaps and ambiguities in the arms control agreements of the 1970s to deploy large numbers of gray area and shorter range systems including the highly accurate, mobile, triple-warhead SS-20 missiles. These inter-mediate-range missiles, which were developed during the height of detente, represent a totally unprovoked major increase in the Soviet nuclear threat to its neighbors. Capable of striking all of Western Europe--and nearly all of Asia as well--from bases within the Soviet Union, they clearly are designed to fulfill the long-standing Soviet objective of dividing Europe from North America.

In response to this development, NATO decided in 1979 to counter the Soviet buildup with a two-tracked program. The first track called for the limited deployment of United States intermediate-range missiles beginning in 1983 and proceeding through 1986. At the same time, NATO called on the Soviet Union to negotiate mutual limitations on these missiles. During the period that we were negotiating, the Soviets deployed over 300 new warheads, while the United States reduced the number of nuclear warheads in Europe by 1,000. We have also an-nounced further unilateral reductions of 1,400 warheads in Europe. In addition, for each of the 572 warheads we may eventually have to deploy should the Soviets fail to negotiate, we are removing an existing warhead from our European stockpiles. Thus, while we reduce the number of nuclear weapons in Europe by a total of 2,400 warheads, the Soviets continue to add to the number of SS-20 missiles deployed in Europe.

In the Intermediate-range Nuclear Force (INF) talks, the United States negotiated patiently and flexibly for two years. President Reagan's "zero option" was designed to eliminate this entire class of nuclear weapons. The Soviets refused our proposal, but it remains on the table. We also have offered an interim proposal whereby both sides would limit their INF deployments to an equal number of warheads below NATO's planned level of 572. The Soviets have thus far refused this proposal as well. Despite our repeated efforts to meet Soviet concerns, Moscow rejected any outcome which would allow the deployment of a single United States missile, while insisting on retaining a formidable SS-20 arsenal for itself in both Europe and Asia. Only then did we begin deployment of Pershing II and cruise missiles. In the two years of our negotiations, during which the Soviets continued to deploy SS-20 missiles at a steady rate, they followed a negotiating strategy which relied on convincing the Europeans that NATO deployments could lead to war, or at least to a drastic cooling in East-West relations. By doing so the Soviets hoped to split the NATO Alliance and thereby prevent the West from redressing the balance. When that kind of intimidation and coercion failed, they walked away from the negotiating table.

The fact that the Soviets have resisted an equitable INF agreement only underscores the point that our efforts to ensure the future cannot rest on arms control alone. Without the NATO deployment program, which is in progress, we would now find ourselves with nothing to offset the massive Soviet superiority in longer-range INF missiles. We would, of course, have preferred it if the Soviets had agreed to negotiate seriously when we proposed the zero option or the interim agreement. We are disappointed by their unjustified and irresponsible decision to leave the talks. We have repeatedly expressed our willingness to remove deployed Pershing II and ground-launched cruise missiles (GLCMs) once an agreement is reached. We and our allies will not make unilateral concessions to convince the Soviets to return to the negotiating table. The United States will, however, negotiate flexibly when they do return. We are prepared to do so immediately.

A sound balance of arms control and modernization has also been the basis of our approach to the Strategic Arms Reduction Talks, commonly known as START. We have proposed deep cuts in deployed missiles and their warheads, with particular emphasis on reductions in land-based ballistic missiles, whose large numbers and short flight times pose special problems for assured crisis stability. Modernization was recommended by the bipartisan Scowcroft Commission, which called for the deployment of 100 MX missiles and the development of a small single-warhead ICBM. These programs are to be integrated with a conscientious arms control effort. The Commission's final report makes clear that all three elements are essential to long-term success. The Administration is committed to carrying out this program and has structured its START proposal to take the Commission's recommendations into account.

We have added further flexibility to our START position by offering to explore specific trade-offs in areas of comparative United States and Soviet advantage. In response to stated Soviet concerns about air-launched cruise missiles (ALCMs), we have proposed levels below those provided for in SALT II. We have shown flexibility in dealing with the destructive capability of missiles. To increase the incentives to shift to more stabilizing strategic deployments, we offered a "build-down" concept that had been framed in close consultations with Congress: each side would eliminate more weapons than it deploys, with the ratio of reductions geared to enhance stability. In reply, the Soviets terminated the negotiations.

Suspension of these negotiations has not increased the danger of nuclear conflict. As President Reagan has said time and again, a nuclear war cannot be won and must never be fought. Nuclear war remains extremely unlikely and will remain so as long as we maintain a sound deterrent. In my judgment, this suspension of the talks is motivated less by differences in substance than by a Soviet belief that the USSR has more to gain in the near term from intimidation than from agreements.

Still, we want to negotiate. We are committed to serious arms control negotiations. As the President has said, everything is on the table. What we need now is for the Soviets to come back. I am convinced that sooner or later the Soviets will find their way back to the nuclear arms negotiations. When they do, they will find us willing and flexible. We have completed a thorough review of our policies. We are ready.

A Conventional Dialogue

Our efforts to achieve meaningful arms control have not been confined to the now-suspended Geneva talks on nuclear arms reductions. In both the Geneva Conference on Disarmament and the Vienna talks on Mutual and Balanced Force Reductions, the United States and its NATO allies have advanced proposals designed to broaden the scope of the East-West arms control agenda. In these areas, our proposals are again aimed at establishing an arms control regime which will enhance Western security, while working to strengthen the foundation of deterrence which has been eroded by Soviet military programs. Here, as in nuclear arms, Western restraint has not been matched by the Soviets.

In 1969, the United States abandoned its biological weapons program and renounced the use of our remaining chemical weapons except in defense. In contrast, the Soviets have continued to build up--and use--their chemical stocks. First introduced during World War I, these horrible weapons have been condemned repeatedly by the world community as being particularly inhumane. Their use in war has been banned by the Geneva Protocol, and a supplementary agreement to ban production, possession or use of related biological and toxin weapons was signed by both the United States and the USSR in 1972. Unfortunately, there is ample evidence that these restraints against chemical weapons are breaking down. Recent Iraqi use of chemical weapons is only the latest and most publicized evidence of this sad fact. Reports of chemical and toxin weapons use by Soviet-aided Communist forces in Southeast Asia go back as far as 1975. The Soviets have also violated the Biological Weapons Convention by their use of toxin weapons in Afghanistan since their invasion in 1979. The steady growth of Soviet chemical warfare capabilities and their apparent willingness to use them only underscores the urgent need to devise and implement an effectively verifiable arms control regime.

In April, Vice President Bush tabled in the Geneva Conference on Disarmament a draft treaty calling for a global, comprehensive ban on the development, production, stockpiling and transfer of chemical weapons. Our draft treaty is the culmination of years of intensive study.

At its heart lie the most thoroughly thought-out verification provisions ever advanced in a single agreement--provisions called for by the concealable nature of chemical weapons stocks and by the ease with which those weapons can be produced. Even a converted warehouse with no outwardly distinguishable signs can be used to store lethal chemical weapons. Our "open invitation" verification provisions for automatic, unimpeded challenge inspection of military and government-owned or controlled facilities are indeed bold, but they are also sound. They have been designed to be as effective as possible so that we and all parties to an eventual agreement can be confident that everyone is honoring its terms. We do not take this proposal lightly. Indeed, everyone involved with security issues realizes that there is some risk associated with opening up our most sensitive military installations to international inspection. Nevertheless, we firmly believe that the chemical weapons problem calls for bold initiatives, and we are prepared to go forth with one. Analogous measures can be taken to assure verification of nuclear testing agreements.

At about the same time that we were presenting our chemical weapons initiative in Geneva, the West presented a new proposal in Vienna aimed at ending the ten-year-old impasse in the MBFR talks on reducing conventional forces in Europe. While both sides agree that the result of negotiations should be parity at lower levels, the East claims that parity already exists. This would imply total Warsaw Pact reductions equal to NATO's. The problem is that the balance of forces in Europe is not equal. By our estimate the East has understated its force levels by more than 200,000 men. To bypass this difficult question, our proposal calls for limiting initial data exchange to combat and combat support forces, which are the most easily identifiable, while postponing consideration of the rear service forces.

The Soviets have publicly criticized both of these proposals, claiming the former are too far-reaching and the latter not far-reaching enough. We hope that when they have had time to study our proposals carefully, the Soviets will offer a more reasoned, constructive response. In Vienna, as in Geneva, we look for signs that the Soviets are prepared to join us in negotiating a serious agreement. But with conventional armaments, as with nuclear, we will not allow our hope for eventual arms control agreements to hold our own defenses hostage.

Future Directions

Last January, in a speech from the White House, President Reagan spoke of his earnest desire to build a constructive relationship with the Soviet Union. Sadly, the Soviets have not yet taken up this offer. The shrill tenor of Soviet statements directed toward the United States has not changed. In addition, while we have shown flexibility in both our INF and START proposals and have promised further flexibility should the Soviets return to Geneva, they still refuse to reestablish the nuclear arms control dialogue.

We believe the Soviets will realize it is in their interest to return to the Geneva talks. We will continue to express our willingness to resume those talks without preconditions. However, broader arms control dialogue and political cooperation with the Soviets cannot be achieved if they are unwilling to take comparable steps to improve our relationship. As President Reagan said in his January speech, "If the Soviet Government wants peace, then there will be peace. Together we can strengthen peace, reduce the level of arms, and know in doing so we have helped fulfill the hopes and dreams of those we represent and, indeed, of people everywhere."

We are fully prepared to resume talks on INF and START, and clearly we would like to move expeditiously toward agreements by the end of 1985. I believe this can be achieved. In such a climate many other arms control initiatives would fall into place. A number of confidence-building measures could be concluded in Stockholm, and cooperation on more effective use of the hot line for prevention of miscalculation may prove possible. Hopefully, we may at last be able to have serious discussions of the means by which we can ensure deterrence and peace well into the next century.

I have described an ambitious agenda, admittedly even an optimistic agenda. I recognize that it may suffer delay in the face of the current Soviet attitude. But if we do not strive, we cannot achieve. The differences between East and West will not disappear in my lifetime, but more importantly, agreement is still possible. I know that the President looks forward to the day when he can meet with his Soviet counterpart personally in a constructive summit. Goodwill on the President's part alone is not sufficient, however. He is also aware that endless concessions, unilateral restraint, and inconsistent policies will not expedite agreement. The United States has put forth fair proposals and is prepared to negotiate. I reiterate the President's message of peace and renew his call for dialogue. We stand ready to build on our relationship. We ask your support in that effort.

CHAPTER 2

STRATEGIC DEFENSE: A CATALYST FOR ARMS REDUCTIONS

by

The Honorable George A. Keyworth, II
Science Advisor to the President,
and Director, Office of Science and
Technology Policy

I have taken as my assignment something that is known by at least two names. In my house we call it the Strategic Defense Initiative, but in most places it goes by the indelible name of "Star Wars." Out of necessity, I have conditioned myself to respond to both.

On March 23, 1983, President Reagan unveiled his Strategic Defense Initiative. It was a thoughtful and comprehensive--and revolutionary--strategy for changing the course of the world to one that promises increased stability against the threat of nuclear weapons.

I would like to share with you why I believe this initiative is so far-reaching in its implications. When we are done I hope I will have convinced you that strategic defense is not, as it is portrayed, a short-sighted program to use modern technology simply to move war into space; nor is it a prelude to a new arms race. It is, in fact, a step towards making the world safer from nuclear weapons.

One of the most frustrating problems of modern times has been the difficulty the two superpowers have faced in finding a workable approach to arms control. We have made distressingly little progress given what are generally assumed to be universal desires to reduce nuclear tension.

If we assume both sides want to reduce tension, why do we find it so difficult to do so? The fact is there are fundamental and practical impediments to arms reductions--impediments that we have to face up to. Like it or not there are profound differences in the two nations' approaches to national defense. The Soviets do not share with us the same logic, cultural values and historical perspectives. We lack a mutually acceptable means to reduce arms.

While the United States and Soviet Union have largely common national security objectives, both countries have fundamentally different ways of enforcing them. We have based our national security on deterrence--the threat of massive nuclear retaliation if the Soviet Union should attack us with nuclear forces. But the Soviet Union seeks its national security goals not through deterrence, but largely through the coercive threat of first-strike. A look at their strategic forces shows that they emphasize the ability to deliver a rapid first-strike as a means of destroying our ability to retaliate. Consider just some of the evidence. Their forces are composed predominantly of heavy, MIRVed ballistic missiles, missiles which, if they are to be of any military use, must be used in the earliest stages of a nuclear war. They are *not* retaliatory weapons. Moreover, the Soviets have been adamant in arms negotiations that they will not weaken their ICBM force, even though it already outnumbers and can outperform ours many times over.

The threat of a Soviet first-strike puts tremendous pressure on our ability to respond quickly with surviving forces. We must maintain thousands of nuclear weapons not, as some people say, to "destroy the world ten times over," but in order that some far smaller number of weapons will survive an enemy's first-strike and be able to retaliate effectively. After all, if the United States is struck without warning, we may find that 90 percent of our ICBMs are destroyed, that most of our bombers are gone, and that perhaps half of our strategic submarine fleet is sunk in port.

So our plans for strategic forces are heavily weighted to maintaining a *survivable*, *retaliatory* capability in the face of improving Soviet strategic forces. And it is this problem of assuring the

18

survivability of our deterrent that gives such high priority to the modernization of our strategic forces. But at the same time we have to recognize that the march of technology makes that task harder and harder each year. Our present deterrent triad--the three-legged stool of land-based missiles, airplanes, and submarines--has become wobbly in recent years. Even the strongest leg, our submarines, while as survivable today as ever, could well be threatened in coming years by the incredibly rapid advances we are seeing these days in data processing technologies. We simply cannot be complacent about the permanence of the triad upon which we have based our national security for decades.

On the other side, the Soviets must perceive that their strategic force, which consists primarily of silo-based ICBMs, will always be vulnerable to modernized U.S. ICBMs. In times of crisis the Soviet Union might then conclude that it *must* strike first. It seems crazy to have a system that becomes so unstable under duress, but their strategic forces have that built-in vulnerability. So the two approaches, ours and the Soviets', are not only fundamentally different, they are also fundamentally unstable when taken together.

There is one additional worry. The Soviets have *not* accepted the inevitability of mutual destruction in the case of nuclear war. They remember their history, and have an abiding belief that Russia, as it has time and time again, will survive to recover. If necessary, they are prepared to fight a protracted nuclear war--and they have taken concrete steps to do so. And a nation that expects to survive a nuclear war has great incentive to try to limit possible damage by knocking out the enemy's strategic weapons first. On the other hand, two generations of Americans have been taught exactly the opposite--that there is no meaningful recovery from nuclear war. We view a first-strike by either side as suicide, and we have arrayed our strategic forces in such a way as to prevent such an action.

So the United States has built a deterrent to maintain peace. We developed what we thought would be enough retaliatory forces to maintain a credible deterrent. On the other side, the Soviet Union built, in effect, a war-fighting machine. They tailored their force--with massive numbers of land-based ICBMs--to inflict crippling damage in preemptive first-strikes. One might characterize our strategy as "to *prevent* a war" and theirs as "in the *event* of war."

This means that in order to make deterrence credible the United States must have enough weapons to ensure survival of a sufficient number of them to retaliate. For preemption, the Soviets must have enough weapons to cripple our deterrent force. We are caught in a spiral of conflicting philosophies. This is why, in arms negotiations, each side places such high priority on protecting their particular weapons--in the Soviets' case the weapons for first-strike, in ours the weapons for retaliation.

We often hear simplistic proposals that each side could reduce its arms by simply limiting the number of warheads with no regard to how they are delivered. But that makes little sense because instability comes not primarily from the numbers of weapons, but instead from how they might be used. That mismatch is also the reason why we cannot, as the *Washington Post* advocates, ". . . simply sit down and rationally negotiate instead of contemplating war in space." We need new options to break the stalemate because the present approaches to deterrence are oil and water. They lack that common denominator that negotiators need.

President Reagan's immediate challenge has therefore been to find and introduce a new and stabilizing factor, something that will permit both the United States and the Soviet Union to reduce their reliance on huge arsenals of nuclear weapons. Strategic defense can be that stabilizing factor. I admit that the introduction of this new factor into what is already a hotly contested arena has certainly not yet brought stability to public debate on arms control. This is not surprising. After all, the President proposed a profound change--a sharp departure from a two generation-old rationale that our safety is assured if each side has the ability to annihilate the other. But the President is far from alone in recognizing the danger in being lulled into a false sense of security.

In fact, he is very much in tune with the motivations driving people throughout the Western world. The nuclear freeze movement, as well as the outspoken pacifism in Europe, both reflect a strong sense that we cannot be assured of the indefinite stability of today's standoff between the nuclear superpowers. That is why he raised the fundamental issue of taking a fresh look at our long-term security.

Not surprisingly, the public and Congress are asking, "Where are we going with this?" Unfortunately, the discussions have too quickly bypassed that central question, and instead have succumbed to detailed analyses of program accounting and cost projections or arguments about technologies that are yet to be developed. Or people insist that all the President really meant was to improve deterrence by defending our Minuteman silos and making it more difficult to neutralize them.

I assure you that none of that was on the President's mind when he made his March 23 speech. Not many people remember that speech for what it was, a vision of how he proposed to approach this broad problem of national security on all fronts. His initial goal is to defuse the most immediately destabilizing threat by making it clear to the Soviets that they can have *no realistic expectations* of launching a successful preemptive strike. But the President's ultimate goal is even more ambitious. It is to reduce the military effectiveness of nuclear weapons so drastically that they become unreliable instruments for modern warfare. At the same time he continues to offer to reduce offensive arms, a prospect that will, partly as a result of strategic defense, become more mutually feasible over time.

One point I should make here is that when we talk today about defense against ballistic missiles--and that is the heart of the current planning for strategic defense--we are *not* talking about the kind of anti-ballistic missile defenses that were discussed in the 1960s. The enormous difference between the opportunities available to us today, compared to those of the 1960s, derives from monumental advances in science and technology. And let me assure you that there are technologies emerging today that we simply could not have anticipated even a few years ago.

The latest example of how far we have come since the 1960s was demonstrated just two weeks ago when the Army tested the first of a new generation of defenses against ballistic missiles. In effect, what they did was hit a bullet with a bullet at a relative speed of more than 20,000 miles per hour. Moreover, the ICBM warhead was stopped at an altitude of about 100 miles before it could reenter the atmosphere. This event proved that it is possible to stop an ICBM with something that is both realistic and thinkable--that is, without using a nuclear weapon. It also previews the arrival of the first generation of ultra-high precision weapons necessary for a comprehensive defense system. Moreover, these recent developments give lie to the critics' assertions that such technologies are "unworkable," "impossible" or "pie-in-the-sky."

These and many other developing technologies that could be relevant to strategic defense were the subject of an intensive study conducted in the half year following the President's speech. Much of that effort was centered on several high-level panels, particularly the panel headed by former NASA head Jim Fletcher.

The Fletcher Panel's overriding conclusion was that we can now project the technology to develop a defense system that could drastically reduce the effectiveness of an attack by ballistic missiles. The key to their conclusion was the feasibility today of something which was not feasible in the earlier ABM debates--and that is destruction of an ICBM in the vulnerable boost phase before its payload has separated into independently targeted warheads. They studied not only defenses against today's missiles, but also against those that could reasonably be expected to be developed in response to such a defense system. They looked at such possible actions as hardening of ICBMs, of spinning them, of shortening the boost phase with fast-burning rockets, of electronic countermeasures and decoys, of numerical proliferation of ICBMs, and many more possibilities. All I can say is that dozens of some of the brightest minds in the United States concluded that any realistic countermeasures the Soviets might attempt would still leave their ICBMs vulnerable to our defenses.

The panel envisioned a system that would very likely consist of several layers of defenses. The system would be designed to attack, first, ballistic missiles during their highly vulnerable and visible boost phases when they are carrying up to ten warheads in a single package; second, warheads during their relatively long mid-course phases when they are coasting high above the atmosphere; and third, warheads during their reentries into the atmosphere.

Let me emphasize the importance of being able to destroy ICBMs during their boost phase because this is what holds so much promise for a revolutionary defense system. It turns out that even a primitive capability to intercept ICBMs during boost phase would give the defender some important options. The introduction of just a limited American strategic defense capability--such as might occur during a period of transition to strategic defense--would force the Soviets to consider that a preemptive first-strike would have uncertain results. This point is critically important. Certainty of success is the *only* basis on which the Soviets would plan to initiate a nuclear attack against the United States.

Some people argue that the Soviets might be so threatened if we began to introduce strategic defense that they might rush to make a preemptive attack against us before our strategic defenses became effective. But this suggestion ignores two facts. First, the Soviets strongly believe in strategic defense and already have a massive ballistic missile defense program underway. I would add that their program benefits from the dedication of some of the Soviets' finest minds. Second, during any transition period both sides would retain their strong ability to retaliate if attacked. Certainly in the intermediate phases the offense would still overcome the defense to convincing degrees in the event of all-out war. My point is that neither the development nor the initial introduction of strategic defense would cause abrupt destabilization. Therefore, American and Soviet national security objectives would be preserved. But--and this is the most important consequence--we will have started to remove the preemptive first-strike as a realistic option. At that point we will have accomplished something that has eluded us for twenty years. We will have effectively eliminated *both* sides' perceptions that the other could launch a successful first-strike. And that finally gives us that common denominator, that long-sought rationale for reducing the size of arsenals.

After all, with the first-strike option removed, nuclear arsenals would then need to be maintained only for retaliatory purposes--that is, in order to keep the other guy honest. But retaliatory arsenals would not have to be nearly as large as arsenals required to survive preemptive strikes in our case, or to launch preemptive strikes in the Soviets' case. Therefore, we would have an opportunity to negotiate greatly reduced arsenals that would still leave each side with a strong retaliatory deterrent.

We would then enter a second transition period during which our defense posture would move toward increased reliance upon conventional, nonnuclear forces. This strengthened role would need to be supported by restoration of technological leverage in the form of traditional force-multipliers that have declined in recent years. At the same time, second- and third-generation defensive technologies and systems would be becoming available. This would further reduce the effectiveness of strategic nuclear weapons.

It is also likely that sometime during this transition period the strategic nuclear forces we are building today would be reaching the limits of their operational lifetimes. We would then have new options for truly great reductions in nuclear arms. We could retire those large obsolete forces and let each side then keep well-protected *token* nuclear arsenals as purely retaliatory deterrents.

I do not offer this scenario lightly. Altering our defense posture under any circumstances is serious. This will force us to rely much more heavily on conventional weapons. Neither our military structure and organization, nor our technology, is ready for it now either strategically or tactically. Strategic defense is not the end-all answer, but it *is* the

24

catalyst.

Finally, let me recapitulate what I think would be the broad outcomes of a successful strategic defense. I have broken these up into two periods of time. One might run from 1985 to 1990. I would characterize that as the period before we make any formal decisions about building a system while we conduct research and development. During this phase we could expect to see some new technical and policy options which, if implemented, would have the following effects.

First, they would cause both sides to think seriously about rejecting the ICBM as a centerpiece of future strategic delivery systems. Second, they would force Soviet planners to rule out an effective first-strike as a realistic option. And third, they would provide American and Soviet arms control negotiators with the common, limited strategic objective of *retaliation* by which to discuss possible build-down of arsenals. What is important to realize is that all of these effects could be stimulated by nothing more than the mutual understanding that both sides were seriously pursuing strategic defense systems.

The second phase, perhaps from 1990 to 2000, would be a time of continued development and initial deployment. At that time we would begin to realize the major *military* capabilities. First, we would negate the ICBM, SLBM, and IRBM as realistic first-strike options against strategic military objectives. Second, we would preferentially defend a limited set of either conventional military systems or populations. Third, we would introduce the capability, if implemented, to defend more effectively against the air-breathing threat of airplanes and cruise missiles. Fourth, we would enforce retaliation as the *sole* rationale for nuclear delivery systems. And, fifth, in light of this balanced deterrence posture, we would provide a means to achieve drastic reductions in the numbers of offensive strategic arms.

All in all, I see each of these developments as monumental achievements. Let me emphasize that strategic defense is not some technical hotshot's idea of how to become a space warrior. Instead, it is our attempt to use the tools we have--modern technology--to rewrite the strategic equations so that we can look forward to a reasonably stable world for generations to come.

PART II

THE IMPACT OF WEAPONS TECHNOLOGY: SPACE AND BEYOND

CHAPTER 3

THE STRATEGIC DEFENSE INITIATIVE

by

Edward T. Gerry
President, W.J. Schafer Associates

My remarks for the session, "Impact of Weapon Technology: Space and Beyond," will center on the President's Strategic Defense Initiative, launched with his speech on March 23, 1983. The primary goal of the Strategic Defense Initiative (SDI) is to provide a path for the stable deterrence of nuclear war into the next century through the introduction of, and increasing dependence on, defensive systems. While a balance of offensive forces has worked so far, the growing numbers and sophistication of ICBM weapons is moving us toward an increasingly less stable situation with advantages to the side that attacks first. Arms control negotiations have not led to reductions or caps on offensive forces primarily because, to be effective, such agreements require some degree of mutual trust or verification which cannot exist at present. On the other hand, deterrence based on defensive systems, properly configured, can be stabilizing. They can also provide for offensive force arms reduction agreements that do not require mutual trust or detailed verification measures in order to be viewed by both sides as in their best interest.

While it is clear that no system made up of technologies that we know about today can guarantee a perfectly leakproof defense, it is extremely important to understand that defensive deterrence does not require a leakproof defense. Defensive deterrence requires only that the defense operate well enough to deny an adversary any confidence that any useful military objective can be achieved through the use of its ballistic missile force. Adequate levels of defense can remove an incentive to a rational adversary for a first-strike, thereby stabilizing the deterrent balance. Defensive deterrence that is stabilizing has two further requirements. First, the defensive systems must be sufficiently survivable so that they cannot be functionally removed prior to an attack. Second, defensive system responses to offense force proliferation must be less costly (by some appropriate measure) than the proliferation of the offense.

If deterrence of nuclear war by whatever means is successful, then the population is completely protected. The previous paragraphs were directed toward making the argument that the addition of defensive options to the policy choices available to future presidents provides for more stable deterrence into the next century and offers a better opportunity for negotiation of meaningful offensive arms limitations. With sufficient defense, the military utility of nuclear weapons could be reduced to the point where they are, in effect, "obsolete." Active pursuit of arms control agreements, in parallel with the development of defensive systems, could very likely hasten the era of "obsolescence."

One additional point needs to be considered, namely, what happens if deterrence fails. Deterrence based on opposing offensive-only forces cannot tolerate even a single serious error. If deterrence should fail through miscalculation or accident, a robust defensive system will greatly reduce the number of civilian deaths. Against small accidental attacks, it may reduce the leakage to zero. Against a massive attack some leakage would likely occur, but there is an enormous difference between ten and 10,000 warheads arriving on United States soil. The institutions and fabric of American society would likely survive an attack of only ten warheads, even though their arrival would be a human tragedy of monumental proportions.

The technological options for implementing an effective defense have become more numerous in recent years. Technology advances over the last twenty years may have made feasible several of those options that seemed beyond reach a decade ago. The Defense Technologies Study (DTS), chaired by Dr. Jim Fletcher, evaluated a wide variety of existing and emerging technologies in the context of a multi-layered defense, recognizing that a layered defense makes the best use of imperfect technologies toward the objective of very low leakage. The DTS identified several combinations of technologies that in a layered deployment would provide low leakage, not only for the current Soviet threat, but for a threat designed to stress the defensive systems. Further, system functional survivability appeared achievable against a variety of attacks, and the possibility appeared real for cost exchange ratios in favor of the defense. These assessments have held up through further analysis since the conclusion of the DTS and they provide the basis for the SDI technology development program. This program supports the policy goal by determining and demonstrating the most suitable technologies to allow an informed decision, as early as possible, on whether to proceed with time phased development and deployment of systems which could evolve into a robust multi-layered defensive system.

The Defense Technologies Study also found that specifying the correct technology goals was critically important to defining a system that was robust to countermeasures and potentially affordable in the long-run. For example, designing a homing rocket vehicle for either midcourse reentry vehicle (RV) intercept or boost-phase intercept with too heavy a homing head drives the size, weight and cost of the system to the point of impracticality. However, modern microelectronics coupled with space-based sensors and designators allow the possibility of a very small, low cost interceptor which might radically change the traditional cost exchange between offense and defense. Similarly, a laser boost-phase system designed at too low a technology level may be vulnerable to retrofit hardening of the ICBM targets, while one designed at the other extreme may be too costly for the extra performance achieved. Further, many of the recent negative arguments on the feasibility of ballistic missile defense (especially involving lasers in the boost phase layer), seem to be based simply on poor choices of technology level, which of course yields poor performance.

In the recent public discussion of the President's Strategic Defense Initiative, far too much emphasis, in my opinion, has been placed on the exotic directed-energy technologies. The technologies that can play a role in the 1990s probably do not include lasers or other directed-energy devices, except in an information transfer, radar or designator role. Directed-energy technologies do, however, provide the growth potential to give long-term viability to the President's initiative well into the next century.

It is important to remember that the current Strategic Defense Initiative program under consideration by Congress is not aimed at developing or deploying a system at all. It is, in fact, a focused technology program which will allow an informed, technologically sound decision on whether a change of strategy for deterrence to include defensive elements is possible and affordable. This information, coupled with parallel policy evaluations, will determine whether such a change is desirable and the best approach for implementing it. I believe that the President's initiative may well prove to be of historic importance. I am optimistic that much of the technology development and demonstrations will be successful and that we will be able to seriously consider a more balanced strategy for deterrence that can maintain stability well into the next century.

CHAPTER 4

REMARKS ON ASAT AND BMD

by

Ashton B. Carter
Research Fellow,
Center for International Studies,
Massachusetts Institute of Technology

Space has a certain allure which is reflected equally in cries that we "must seize the high ground" and that we "must avoid militarizing space." This emotional allure or comic-book aura is not very helpful in perceiving or obtaining the military space programs we need. I prefer to start from the point of view that there is nothing special or dramatic about space. It should be regarded as merely another medium for national security activities. We should apply to it the same standards of cost effectiveness, survivability and trade-offs with alternatives that we apply to our other military decisions. The political drama can be taken into account after we get our bearings in a hardheaded military sense.

So far the superpowers have found it attractive to use space only for the five traditional military support missions of communications, reconnaissance and surveillance, navigation, meteorology and geodesy. This military equipment, located in space, does not differ functionally from a host of other military equipment about which we make much less fuss, such as reconnaissance aircraft, microwave communication towers, and terrestrial navigation beacons like LORAN. I have some trouble understanding the military logic of anti-satellite (ASAT) arms control because it seems peculiar to create a sanctuary in space for this type of military equipment. Why should not satellites be

33

subject to the same vulnerabilities to which all the other instruments of warfare are subject?

But suppose it is politically necessary or desirable, either to supplement other military or arms control initiatives or to channel our own activities and institutions in constructive directions, to arrive at some understanding with the Soviet Union about military uses of space. It seems to me this should be done with full recognition of four realities that result from the fragility and exposed condition of spacecraft.

First, even if the United States and the Soviet Union negotiate an arms control treaty banning dedicated, overt ASAT systems on both sides, we will still need to worry about certain residual threats to some of our spacecraft. For instance, the Soviet Union will presumably still possess boosters and spacecraft with the ability to maneuver precisely in space, including maneuvering to the vicinity of an American spacecraft and then exploding. The Soviets will still have satellite antennas suitable for jamming uplinks. The Soviets will still maintain their ICBMs and the missile defense interceptors they have deployed around Moscow, both of which are capable of climbing to low-earth orbital altitudes and detonating their nuclear warheads in the vicinity of U.S. satellites. We shall have to worry to some degree that somewhere in some shed in the Soviet Union there is a laser--chemical, excimer or free electron-- capable of attacking our satellites in low-earth orbit. Last, we all have to consider that every Soviet spacecraft in orbit--still in use or shut down--might have a fragmentation warhead aboard.

A second point is that because of the fragility of space systems and the possibility of residual threats, we should take strong measures to protect our satellites with or without an arms control treaty. Supporters of ASAT arms control should also support satellite survivability programs which would build into our spacecraft the countermeasures that would make attack on them more difficult (impossible is perhaps too much to ask). This would serve to help disrupt the residual threats the Soviets would or could retain under a treaty. The NAVSTAR Constellation is an unclassified space system that illustrates the kind of measures that are worthwhile at relatively modest cost.

Third, we should avoid dependence on satellites for wartime purposes that is out of proportion to our ability to protect them. If we make ourselves dependent upon spacecraft for vital support missions we will have built an Achilles' heel into our military forces. We need, therefore, to consider less elegant backup systems. For instance, elevated line-of-sight reconnaissance in a NATO war could be provided from aircraft, remotely piloted vehicles, helicopters, sounding rockets, balloons, and so on depending on the circumstance. We have programs of this kind today.

Fourth, and perhaps optionally, we should do everything that the ASAT treaty permits to put Soviet satellites at risk. The reason for this recommendation is that many people worry that Americans obey the spirit of a treaty and refrain from all sorts of activities not explicitly banned. In the nuclear arms talks a little ambiguity and creative interpretation on the Soviets' part, although annoying, in general does not cause great harm. But satellites are few in number and potentially decisive. We should, therefore, persuade ourselves that we will not end up militarily disadvantaged by the arms control treaty.

The last observation I want to make about ASAT is to point out a paradox inherent in signing an ASAT treaty that makes space, in effect, a military sanctuary. The paradox is this: To the extent that arms control suppresses ASAT activities and masks the inherent vulnerability of spacecraft, the two super-powers will be tempted to use space more and more for military support. To the extent they do so, pressures will build for ASATs. For example, if we allow Soviet radar satellites (RORSATs) to track our carriers and direct air attacks against our fleet, our naval commanders are going to insist on an ASAT or some other technique for disrupting RORSATs. Their position is not unreasonable.

Now let me turn to ballistic missile defence (BMD). This is an emotional issue since it touches, or purports to touch, the vital issue of survival. It is politically volatile because the person of the President has become attached to it. BMD has long been--undeservedly--a pariah among strategic subjects. This suppression is undeserved because there really is nothing logical or natural about a strategic environment, such as the one we inhabit, which eschews defence yet pursues a vigorous and seemingly unbounded competition in offensive weapons. I have long thought that BMD should be part of our bag of tricks for improving our strategic posture, especially as I worked on MX basing and on survivability of our strategic C^3I (Command, Control, Communication, and Intelligence). In these areas the preponderance of offense is simply numbing. It makes it awfully difficult to guarantee survivability into the future. We are heavily reliant on strategic defense today, though these defenses are passive. We hide subs, move airborne command posts and bombers, harden silos, proliferate communications nodes, and so on. Why not add active defenses to these familiar techniques?

What everyone wants to know about BMD, of course, is "Does it work?" I think it is very important in answering this question to specify *carefully*, "Work for what purpose?" There are a number of militarily sound goals for BMD including protecting our retaliatory forces, protecting other military targets, and frustrating or confusing attacks that aim at well-defined military objectives. Each of these goals imposes different technical requirements. It is possible that some of them can be satisfied soon, and without resort to controversial space-based components.

It is a little embarrassing to have to turn from these military goals to another goal--the most ambitious goal of all--of building something like a perfect or damage-denying defense. Such a defense would literally remove from the hands of the Soviet Union the ability to do dreadful damage to our society with nuclear weapons. It would allow us to pursue with impunity activities that might otherwise provoke them into such an act. My own judgment--and it is a matter of judgment, not proof, though some judgments can be very firm--is that the prospect for fashioning such a defense is so remote (more in probability than in time) that BMD cannot be a sensible basis for public expectation or national policy.

The reasons for this judgment are several. One must think the problem through and say *why* you agree or disagree with this judgment, rather than appealing to some vague Murphy's Law. But the important point to grasp is that a damage-denying defense does not so much differ from a less-than-perfect defense in magnitude as in kind. An enemy trying to preserve the elemental threat of crippling our society can do many more things to sidestep a damage-denying defense than an enemy trying to preserve a larger menu of strategic options in the face of a less-than-perfect defense.

We are all obliged to address (or take pains to finesse) this extreme goal because the claims for BMD in the political arena have been getting more grandiose. It is easy to understand and sympathize with this trend. After a few years of racetrack versus densepack, and a few more of warhead limits versus throw-weight limits, you begin to say to yourself, "All this is just tinkering at the margin of the nuclear dilemma. Isn't there something more dramatic we can do?" This cry echoes the cry of the freeze movement, the Catholic bishops and others asking fundamental questions today about the nuclear puzzle. On the other hand, to those frustrated with the lack of patience, continuity and sense of purpose in United States strategic planning in the past decade--the kind of frustration expressed by the Scowcroft Commission--this casting about for dramatic alternatives is disappointing.

To conclude, I believe that BMD might become a fitting component of, or complement to, our overall strategic outlook, but it cannot serve as a replacement for that outlook. It is not a grand solution. The search for a grand solution will divert attention from the real opportunities we have to improve our strategic situation.

This reminds me of the case of the religious man trapped in the floods of this spring. He was standing ankle-deep in water on his porch when a canoe came by. The man in the canoe said, "Hop in. They say the water is going to keep rising." But the religious man said, "No thanks. I have faith in the Lord, and I'm staying where I am." The canoes paddled off. Before long the man was leaning out his second floor window, and again ankle-deep in water. A canoe passed by the window, and its occupant offered, "Hop in. They say the water will keep rising." "No, I have faith in the Lord, and I'm staying right where I am." The canoe departed. The religious man was standing on his roof, ankle-deep in water, when a motorboat came by, "Hop in, I'll take you to safety. They say the water is still rising." "No, I have faith in the Lord, and I'll stay right here," replied the religious man. Before long, the man was standing on the chimney, and the water flowed around his ankles. A helicopter approached and hovered overhead. A helmeted head leaned out and shouted, "Grab this rope and we'll take you away. The water is going to keep rising." But the religious man hollered back, "No thanks. I have faith in the Lord." The man in the helmet shook his head, the rope ascended, and the helicopter flew away.

Pretty soon the religious man was standing before the Pearly Gates, and he was madder than hell. He said to Saint Peter, "What happened? I had faith in the Lord." And Peter replied, "Look, what do you want? We sent you two canoes, a motorboat, and a helicopter!"

The search for the grand solution diverts us from those many small acts of insight and intelligent efforts that are our real salvation.

CHAPTER 5

NEW WEAPONS TECHNOLOGY: THE CHALLENGE FOR ARMS CONTROL

by

Frank J. Gaffney, Jr.
Deputy Assistant Secretary of Defense,
Strategic and Nuclear Forces

This paper will focus on the broad questions of the challenge that changing weapons technologies present to arms control. It will also examine how our requirements for technologically advanced systems affect our needs, ambitions and aspirations for arms control. The views I will present are my own. They do not necessarily reflect Administration policy, but are born of several years experience working in both the Congress and the Executive Branch on nuclear arms control and force modernization policy issues.

Most of the nuclear policy issues that now face the legislative and executive branches of the government raise concerns about the impact of technological change on our overall national security needs and about the status and future of arms control. Those questions are a primary focus, for example, of the recent congressional debates over the MX/Peacekeeper intercontinental ballistic missile (ICBM), the U.S. program to develop an anti-satellite (ASAT) capability, the sea-launched cruise missile (SLCM), the ratification of the Threshold Test Ban Treaty and proposals for a Comprehensive Test Ban Treaty.

The same concerns arise in the two-fold Executive Branch examination of existing and possible future arms control agreements. In the first place, we are carefully monitoring and assessing the impact of existing agreements, including the pattern of Soviet compliance with them. In the course of that assessment, we have been forced to confront the reality of the shortcomings of many of those agreements: definitional and language problems, ambiguities, loopholes, substantive lacunae, inadequate verification provisions, etc. We have also been forced to confront the reality of Soviet noncompliance with a range of past arms control agreements. After careful review, the Executive Branch concluded early this year that the Soviet Union had committed violations and probable violations of legal obligations and political commitments in seven areas initially studied, including the 1925 Geneva Protocol, the 1972 Biological Warfare Convention, the 1972 Anti-Ballistic Missile (ABM) Treaty, the 1974 Threshold Test Ban Treaty, the 1975 Helsinki Final Act and the 1979 SALT II Treaty.

The Executive Branch has also been working on a variety of possible future arms control agreements. We tabled far-reaching proposals for deep cuts in nuclear weaponry in the Strategic Arms Reductions Talks (START) and in the negotiations on intermediate-range nuclear forces (INF). Unfortunately, the Soviet government suspended both talks at the end of 1983, but the United States is ready to resume them at any time without preconditions. In addition, we are studying a range of possible options for space arms control--an area in which the challenges posed by modern weapons technology are particularly apparent. Major verification difficulties, the variety of threats to United States and allied satellites, and the military importance of Soviet targeting and reconnaissance satellites complicate the search for effective space arms control measures.

All of these deliberations on nuclear force modernization and arms control focus on the critical question of how to meet our security requirements in light of the changing national security picture, the changing challenges to arms control and the changing experience we have with arms control. Not all of those changes derive from technological advances, but many of the most important among them do. I would therefore like to suggest five tenets that I hope would be of use in our collective--congressional, Executive and public--consideration of this difficult and troubling area.

First, like it or not, we must recognize that arms control agreements cannot constrain technological change if any party to the negotiations wishes to see such technology unconstrained. The first effort at nuclear arms control amply illustrates the point. In 1946, the United States presented the Baruch Plan to outlaw all nuclear weapons and place nuclear technology under international authority. Having acquired that technology, the United States was prepared to give it up. It quickly became apparent, however, that the Soviet Union was not willing to consider the Baruch Plan as long as it could not obtain comparable technological capabilities.

Similarly, the 1972 SALT I Interim Agreement on Offensive Forces froze the number of intercontinental ballistic missile launchers, but not warhead levels. Thus, it placed no limits on the parties' ability to exploit the then-emerging MIRV (multiple independently targetable reentry vehicle) technology. The 1972 Anti-Ballistic Missile Treaty limited deployment of ABM systems, but permitted research in new ABM technologies. The lesson is clear. Arms control cannot impose significant constraints on advances in weapons technology, unless both parties are willing to accept those limits.

Second, qualitative advantages of a military nature remain the bedrock of American security. For quite some time the United States has sought to counter quantitative disadvantages with technological superiority. For example, from the time that we demobilized at the end of the Second World War, we chose to offset Warsaw Pact conventional force superiority with our nuclear deterrent. When Soviet nuclear forces acquired several important quantitative advantages, we hoped to balance those with qualitative advances. Thus, we worked on MIRVed systems, accuracy improvements and quieting techniques for our strategic submarines. More recently, we have been engaged in the pursuit of so-called "stealth" technology in an effort to ensure the continued effectiveness of our air-breathing systems.

The number, qualitative magnitude and military significance of the advantages obtained by the United States have been changing dramatically of late. The Soviet Union has made major advances in submarine quieting, anti-submarine warfare (ASW), ICBM accuracy and survivability, long-range cruise missiles, air defenses and even in such unthinkable areas as chemical and biological warfare capability. This multi-faceted Soviet technological progress is having a dramatic impact on the military balance. It poses serious challenges to the continued effectiveness of our deterrent. We are increasingly looking toward a day when the United States will not enjoy the technological lead on which we have relied in the past.

Third, American unilateral restraint in the development and acquisition of new technologies does not appear to be a critical determinant for Soviet decisions about their own acquisition programs. Any number of examples illustrate this important point. I will cite just a few of them.

1. The United States canceled its ground-based anti-satellite program in the 1970s. Consequently, the Soviet Union has maintained the world's only operational ASAT interceptor for about a dozen years.

2. For the first time since the 1950s, the United States began to deploy sea-launched cruise missiles in 1984. The Soviet Union has since the 1960s fielded large numbers of nuclear- and conventionally-armed SLCMs offering a wide assortment of offensive capabilities.

3. The USSR began deploying longer-range intermediate-range (INF) missiles which could strike our European and Asian allies and friends in the late 1950s. Although the United States withdrew its comparable missiles from Europe in the early 1960s, the USSR began fielding the modern, triple-warhead SS-20 longer-range INF missile in the western and eastern USSR in 1977. That force now numbers 378 missiles

with more than 1,100 warheads, and it is still growing.

4.   The United States has not manufactured any new chemical weapons since 1969, and fully complies with the prohibition of the 1972 Biological Weapons Convention against the production or stockpiling of biological weapons. The Soviet Union appears to have developed biological weapons and has an enormous modern chemical weapons capability. Moreover, it has used, or supported the use of, chemical agents and toxins weapons in Afghanistan and Southeast Asia in violation of both the 1972 Convention and the 1925 Geneva Protocol.

Fourth, the problem of attempting to constrain qualitative weapons improvements through arms control is compounded by the fact that those improvements are inherently difficult to verify. An excellent case in point is our effort in the SALT II Treaty to obtain significant constraints on ICBM modernization, primarily through a prohibition on more than one new type of ICBM. The SS-X-25 that the USSR is now developing is in every respect a prohibited second new type, but the Soviets have sought to exploit existing verification uncertainties--and create new ones through measures like encryption of telemetry--in order to argue that the new ICBM is a permitted modernization of an existing type.

The final tenet is both the central one and perhaps the most difficult for the average person to grasp. Technological advances may make the task of arms control as we have known it--and I emphasize "as we have known it"--more difficult. But it may, nonetheless, be the case that such technological improvements actually serve to enhance the purposes that arms control is intended to serve: stability, maintenance of an effective deterrent to war and preservation of peace.

In conclusion, I would like to discuss briefly the implications of these five tenets as I see them and as I believe the Administration sees them. We have concluded that it is imperative to emphasize in our research, development and acquisition programs the development and deployment of those technologies needed for our security. In doing so, we have given--and will continue to give--full consideration to the compatibility of such technologies with arms control as we have known it. It is essential to remember, however, that arms control is a means to an important end, rather than an end in itself. The decision to proceed with acquiring advanced military technologies should therefore be predicated primarily upon a judgment about whether they will promote the *goals* of arms control, rather than simply on their compatibility with the kinds of arms control approaches with which we are familiar.

I believe that the Congress of the United States, the Scowcroft Commission and the Administration have embraced this larger principle in a bipartisan and most important way. A leading example is the small ICBM program that was recommended by the Scowcroft Commission. Most experts and laymen will appreciate that the small ICBM--which might be mobile and deployed in relatively large numbers compared to the MX, and which is currently prohibited by the SALT II Treaty--could pose significant problems to arms control as we have known it. But the small ICBM is hardly incompatible with the *purposes* of arms control. On the contrary, there is broad bipartisan agreement that the small ICBM may greatly increase strategic stability by reducing the value of each strategic target, and thus move away from the destabilizing threat posed by MIRVed ICBMs.

Other modernization programs which represent different areas of technological progress--anti-satellite weapons, cruise missiles, the Strategic Defense Initiative--are more controversial. We should carefully consider, however, the extent to which these programs will advance the purpose of arms control even as they may pose difficulties for earlier arms control approaches. These programs may signal the beginning of a new era that is more stable, secure and, ultimately, more peaceful than the one we now know.

In short, I believe technological progress is

inevitable. The challenge facing us today and in the years to come is for us to exploit its potential for stabilizing the strategic balance. If we are successful in this effort, technology can complement our arms control initiatives and, in a synergistic fashion, work toward a common objective: increasing the disincentives for aggression and promoting the prospects for lasting peace.

PART III

START AND INF:
THE SEARCH FOR EAST-WEST STABILITY

CHAPTER 6

ARMS CONTROL POLICY STABILITY AND COMPLIANCE

by

Keith B. Payne
Executive Vice President and
Director of National Security Studies,
National Institute for Public Policy

The Soviet walkout of the INF talks and the hiatus in the START negotiations provides an opportunity to examine some of the fundamental tenets of arms control. Unfortunately, arms control debates in the United States tend to focus upon details of various designs and proposals prior to consideration of preliminary and basic issues. For example, the important but side issues of negotiability and verification often take precedence over more basic issues such as an identification of the arms control objectives being pursued and how various proposed arms control regimes specifically might contribute to the achievement of those objectives. The classic arms control objectives are:[1]

1. To reduce the probability of war;

2. To reduce the destructiveness of war;

3. To minimize the cost of maintaining an adequate military establishment.

Unfortunately, how various arms control proposals might support any of these objectives in the long-run is understood poorly. For example, it is extremely difficult to known how to pursue the first goal of arms control, i.e., to reduce the probability of war. This is the case not only because of the usual difficulties associated with tough negotiations, but more importantly because of the very modest understanding of the causes of war and peace. Hypotheses concerning war causation abound, yet there is no consensus in support of a general theory of war causation. Historical case studies have been used to support a variety of different, sometimes conflicting, theories of war causation.[2] And fortunately, there is an absence of historical data to assist in establishing a clear understanding of the causes of the bilateral use of nuclear weapons. Suffice it to say, we are far short from understanding the combinations of political and military conditions that will lead to nuclear war or, conversely, to the absence of nuclear war. Once the self-evident factors of existing political conflict and the possession of nuclear weapons are listed, our understanding of nuclear war causation becomes inherently murky.

This problem becomes severe when any attempt is made to establish an arms control regime that will enhance stability, i.e., to reduce the probability of war. The inherent limitation in our understanding of war and peace causation means that any proposed structuring or restructuring of the strategic balance through arms control can have only a highly questionable effect upon the probability of war.

The cavalier fashion in which the words "stabilizing" or "destabilizing" are applied to various arms control proposals and weapons systems belies the fact that there can be no confident predictions concerning what is, or is not, "stabilizing." Our level of understanding does not warrant any such prediction although they are made often. Note, for example, that the Kennedy-Hatfield "Freeze Proposal" of 1982 (Senate Joint Resolution 163) claims that a freeze would help "to reduce the risk of nuclear war." Similarly, the Preamble of the 1972 Anti-Ballistic Missile (ABM) Treaty claims that limitations on such defensive systems would reduce the probability of war. Rarely is it acknowledged that a confident basis for making any such predictions does not exist. Any claim concerning how to reduce the probability of war must be based upon an assumed understanding of what causes war or peace. Yet there is no consensus concerning a theory or theories that can provide that understanding. The great difficulty of marshalling clear evidence in support of such a theory cautions against any statements of certainty concerning whether a proposed arms control regime will be stabilizing. Indeed, if an arms control arrangement actually contributed to stability we would likely be unaware of its beneficial effect. It would be difficult if not impossible to discern the degree to which the probability of war had been reduced, or precisely why it had been reduced.

The severe inadequacy of existing theory to explain or predict war causation in general and nuclear war causation in particular does not mean that we simply should give up efforts to reduce the probability of war through arms control. However, it does mean that there is very little clear guidance to inform us concerning how force structures *should* be affected through negotiations in pursuit of the first goal of arms control.

There are indeed various hypotheses concerning how the probability of nuclear war might be reduced. Unfortunately, these hypotheses have little more than intuition and extremely elementary deductive logic upon which to base their validity. For example, the prevalent model of nuclear war causation which has provided the theoretical basis for U.S. strategic deterrence and arms control policy is predicated upon two assumptions. First, vulnerable strategic forces increase the probability of nuclear use by placing a premium on preemption. Second, the condition of mutually vulnerable societal assets reduces the probability of war by placing a high anticipated cost on the first-use of strategic nuclear weapons.

Ironically, the American approach to strategic arms control stemming from this prevalent "theory" of stability has worked directly *against* the second objective of arms control, i.e., reducing the destructiveness of war. The U.S. approach to SALT I was dominated by an attempt to formalize deterrence stability based upon a condition of mutual societal vulnerability and retaliatory force survivability. The

ABM Treaty in particular reflects an effort to codify a condition of stability predicated upon societal vulnerability. Such an approach to arms control may serve to reduce the probability of war *if* the particular notion that vulnerability ensures stability is valid (something that cannot be known), but it certainly does not provide a negotiating orientation that could facilitate a reduction in the destructiveness of war should it occur.

In contrast to the United States' approach to arms control in SALT I, it is likely (but again cannot be proven) that the *deployment* of ballistic missile defenses (BMD) and other strategic defenses, when complemented by limitations on offensive forces (if possible), would be supportive of the first arms control objectives of reducing the probability of war. Also, it almost certainly would support the second objective of arms control, i.e., reducing the destructiveness of war should it occur. This brief forum is not an appropriate place for a long review of the reasoning behind this claim, although the basic chain of logic has been presented elsewhere.[3]

In regard to more specific arms control considerations, it certainly appears to be the case that now would not be an appropriate time to sign or ratify any additional arms control measures (e.g., an ASAT agreement) that require a strict standard of verification. This is because the issue of Soviet noncompliance with existing agreements and commitments is yet to be resolved. To formalize any additional arms control commitment or agreement after officially declaring, but not resolving, the problem of Soviet noncompliance would send an unfortunate message to Moscow. It would establish or reinforce the perspective in Moscow that the United States condones known and officially declared Soviet arms control violations. Such a Soviet perspective would severely undercut the basis for any future useful arms control agreements. If the United States appears resistent to enforcing compliance for whatever reason, then the entire issues of compliance with limitations that require verification will appear to be a charade. Useful arms control agreements could not be achieved under such a shadow.

The question of whether Soviet violations are "militarily significant" is not at issue at this point. What is critical is that the Soviet Union understands that the United States is serious about the necessity of Soviet compliance with commitments.

Obviously, the Soviet walkout of INF and the absence of START render negotiations during the current period problematic in any event. If the Soviet Union exhibits an increased willingness to resume negotiations, the United States should not hesitate to engage in a serious dialogue. However, it should also make clear that no agreement could be reached until issues of noncompliance are resolved and Soviet violations cease. Some of the unacceptable Soviet practices can be identified. They have been presented officially and publicly. While there have been numerous allegations of repeated Soviet arms control violations, this review will focus only upon those presented by President Reagan.

On January 23, 1984, President Reagan delivered to Congress his "Report on Soviet Noncompliance With Arms Control Agreements." This report cited seven noncompliance issues which are reviewed briefly below.[4]

First, the President's report found that the Soviet Union repeatedly violated the 1972 Biological and Toxin Weapons Convention and the 1925 Geneva Protocol by maintaining an offensive biological warfare program and through its involvement in the use of chemical agents in Laos, Kampuchea and Afghanistan. Second, the Soviet Union violated the 1975 Helsinki Final Act of the Conference on Security and Cooperation by providing inadequate prior notification of the Zapad-81 military exercise. Third, Soviet deployment of a new, large phased-array radar at Krasnoyarsk in central Siberia "almost certainly constitutes" a violation of the 1972 ABM Treaty. The fourth, fifth and sixth issues of noncompliance concern the superpowers' agreement to abide by the signed but unratified SALT II Treaty. Soviet behavior has raised noncompliance concerns in three areas: violation of the prohibition on impeding treaty verification through the encryption of missile test telemetry; "probable violation" of the prohibition on the testing of a second new ICBM by its testing of the new SS-X-25 ICBM; and, the "probable violation" of the SALT II prohibition on the deployment of the SS-16 type ICBM. Finally, Soviet nuclear testing activities constitute a "likely violation" of the terms of the 1974 Threshold Test Ban Treaty.

The Soviet response to the President's Report on Soviet Noncompliance came on January 29, 1984 when the Soviet Embassy in Washington presented an aide-memoire to the State Department. The Soviet aide-memoire did not respond to the American charges; rather it contained countercharges of United States noncompliance. The Soviet note consisted primarily of general criticisms of the U.S. strategic modernization program and the strategic defense initiative. The few specific charges in the Soviet aide-memoire were rebutted two days later in a point-by-point response by the State Department. The specifics of the President's report contrasts sharply with the generality of the Soviet aide-memoire.

Subsequent to this exchange of charges the President has reconfirmed Soviet violation of arms control agreements.[5] It also has been reported that in addition to the encryption of missile telemetry data cited in the President's report, the Soviet Union has engaged in electronic jamming of American satellites and radar systems used to monitor Soviet arms control compliance (or noncompliance). Such a practice would constitute a violation of SALT I and SALT II. This jamming may have occurred since the fall of 1983 during selected Soviet missile flight tests. United States telemetry monitoring satellites, the Cobra Dane missile monitoring radar in the Aleutians and other monitoring radars reportedly have been jammed selectively by the Soviet Union in an effort to conceal data on Soviet surface-to-air and ABM systems.[6] Soviet jamming of U.S. monitoring satellites was confirmed recently in congressional testimony by Richard Perle, Assistant Secretary of Defense for International Security Policy.[7]

Additional data on Soviet noncompliance may soon be forthcoming. An unclassified version of a classified report by ACDA's General Advisory Committee on

Arms Control may soon be available. This report is entitled, "A Quarter Century of Soviet Compliance Practices Under Arms Control Commitments: 1958 -1983 (U)" (dated November 1984). The study reportedly confirms and details seventeen Soviet arms control violations.[8]

The point here is not simply to bemoan Soviet noncompliance with existing arms control agreements, but to suggest that until American concerns are resolved and the Soviet Union discontinues its violations, the United States should not consent to any additional arms control agreements that require careful monitoring of compliance. Virtually any anti-satellite (ASAT), START, INF, test ban or MBFR agreement would necessitate strict verification standards. Concluding new agreements before addressing Soviet noncompliance with existing commitments could only undercut the value of the new agreement and any future negotiations and agreements.[9]

Summary and Conclusion

Arms control debates in the United States focus so closely on details that the forest often is lost for the trees. The current and perhaps short-lived hiatus in strategic arms control negotiations should be used to step back and examine some of the fundamentals of arms control. What specific results should the United States pursue through negotiations, and how are those results related to the ultimate objectives of arms control? For example, how might any restructuring of the strategic balance through arms control reduce the probability of war? A second area requiring attention is how the United States will react to discovery of Soviet noncompliance with arms control commitments. If the United States cannot bring itself to confront, much less address, the question of "After Detection-- What?",[10] it has no business engaging in arms control agreements requiring strict standards of verification. Sufficient evidence of Soviet noncompliance has been accumulated to lead to official charges of cheating. These concerns have not been resolved and Soviet violations appear to be continuing.

The most helpful step that the United States could make at this time in support of arms control would be to take a wider than usual perspective and attempt to find and identify the forest before negotiating about the trees.

ENDNOTES

[1] For the classic treatment of the objectives of arms control see Donald G. Brennan, "Setting and Goals of Arms Control," in *Arms Control, Disarmament, and National Security*, Donald G. Brennan, ed. (New York, George Braziller, 1961), pp. 19-42.

[2] For an interesting compilation of war causation theories see, Leon Branson and George Goethals, War: Studies from *Psychology, Sociology, Anthropology* (New York: Basic Books Inc., 1968).

[3] See Keith B. Payne and Colin S. Gray, "Nuclear Policy and the Defense Transition," *Foreign Affairs*, Vol. 62, No. 4 (Spring 1984), pp. 820-842.

[4] The President's report, reprinted in *Congressional Record Senate*, February 1, 1984, pp. S648-649.

[5] See, "President's News Conference on Foreign and Domestic Issues," *New York Times*, June 15, 1984, p. 12.

[6] This possible arms control violation is discussed in, "Pentagon refuses to deny report on Soviet jamming," *Washington Times*, June 8, 1984, p. 4; and "Soviets Jamming U.S. Satellites and Monitoring Radars," *Soviet Aerospace*, Vol. 41, No. 6 (June 11, 1984), pp. 35-36.

[7] See Walter Andrews, "Defense Aide Confirms U.S. Satellites Jammed," *Washington Times*, June 21, 1984, p. 1.

[8] See the discussions in, *Congressional Record House*, May 31, 1984, pp. H-5087-H-5088; and *Congressional*

Record-Senate, June 19, 1984, pp. S-7597-S-7599.

[9] For an excellent assessment of the issue of Soviet noncompliance see, Colin S. Gray, "U.S. Policy and Soviet Arms Control Violations--Actions Not Words," *Foreign Policy* (Forthcoming, Fall 1984).

[10] Fred Ikle, "After Detection--What?" *Foreign Affairs*, Vol. 39, No. 2 (January 1961), pp. 209-220.

CHAPTER 7

THE UNRAVELING OF ARMS CONTROL

by

John B. Rhinelander
Shaw, Pittman, Potts & Trowbridge

The title of our panel discussion, "START and INF:
Search for East-West Stability," suggests that stability
starts with arms control. That has clearly not been
the case in the past and will not be so in the future.
Constructive negotiations on arms control require an
acceptable order in the overall relationship between
the United States and the USSR.

But even if the general relationship were to improve
over the near term, or arms control were one factor
in improving relations, we can no longer assume that
the arms control focus will be on offensive weapons
systems subject to the recent discussions at START
and INF.

Before March 23, 1983, when the President gave his
"Star Wars" speech, the unstated premise of negotia-
tions since 1972--specifically, the Vladisvostock
Accord, the 1979 SALT II Treaty, and the START/
INF negotiations--rested on the assumption that
defensive strategic systems would remain under limits.
The task was to continue the search for controls of
offensive systems.

This is no longer the case. The President has
announced a demonstration program flatly inconsistent
with the 1972 Anti-Ballistic Missile (ABM) Treaty.
Over the next four years, the Strategic Defense
Initiative (SDI) will at least in some respects, such as
the testing of the Talon Gold program from the Space
Shuttle in 1987 and 1988, violate the ABM Treaty if
pursued as presently formulated. The purpose of SDI

as announced by the President is to develop and demonstrate weapons-related technologies and capabilities which are explicitly prohibited by the ABM Treaty.

Briefly, the ABM Treaty prohibits either side from deploying a nationwide ABM system or even a base for such a system. As amended by the 1974 Protocol, the Treaty limits both sides to a single ABM site in defense of either its capital or an ICBM deployment area. The Treaty specifically prohibits development, testing or deployment of space-based ABM systems or components. In fact, it prohibits any ABM system or component which is not fixed and land-based.

It is true that all arms control treaties should be periodically reviewed and amended as appropriate with changing technologies. It is also true that in the case of the ABM Treaty there are many critical ambiguities which require agreed interpretation between the Soviets and the United States. Finally, there are current, serious compliance issues involving both the USSR and the United States.

I will list a few problem areas to illustrate the nature of the problems under the Treaty:

Large Phased-Array Radars

In negotiating the ABM Treaty we were not able to construct a fully satisfactory regime to deal with the complex problems of large phased-array radars. This type of radar can serve many different purposes. In my judgment the construction of the Soviet radar near Krasnoyarsk in Siberia is a violation of Article VI(b) of the Treaty. However, the American PAVE PAWS early warning radars, which are under construction in Georgia and Texas, raise issues of compliance under the same Article VI(b), which requires early warning radars to be on the nation's periphery and oriented outward. The Soviets claim the Krasnoyarsk radar is not for early warning, but for space-tracking. This explanation is not credible.

The two new PAVE PAWS radars are arguably on the periphery of the United States, but they are not necessarily oriented outward because each radar has

240 degree coverage. Surprisingly, State Department and ACDA officials I talked to were previously unaware of the issue. These are only two of the phased-array radar issues which require further negotiations to prevent continuing allegations of violations and undermining of the Treaty.

Article VI(a) of the Treaty prohibits giving non-ABM systems capabilities to counter strategic ballistic missiles.

While the principal focus of the Nixon Administration during the negotiation of SALT I was on surface-to-air missiles (SAM), Article VI(a) is not limited to SAMs. Its prohibitions apply equally to anti-tactical missiles (ATMs) and anti-satellite missiles (ASATs). The term "capability," as used in Article VI(a), has not been defined, and should be interpreted according to some rule of reason. Nevertheless, the ABM Treaty is coming under increasing pressure as new SAMs and ATMs are built with inherently greater ABM capability, particularly against submarine-launched ballistic missiles (SLBMs).

Space Based and "Future" Systems

There are a bundle of terms in the ABM Treaty which have not been defined which are directly relevant to space-based systems using new technology: "develop," "component," "adjunct," "substitute for," and "perform the function of." These terms are at the heart of the prohibitions dealing with developing and testing space-based systems. Because they are not defined, they offer room for the United States in the first instance, and the Soviet Union later, to suggest legal arguments that various activities are not in fact prohibited by the Treaty. The Homing Overlay Experiment (HOE) program raises current issues. Talon Gold will raise problems in 1986-1988.

One approach the Department of Defense is now using for the Strategic Defense Initiative program is to label ABM-capable systems as "ASATs." Another technique is to call devices "adjuncts," which are permitted under the terms of the ABM Treaty. These approaches are similar in nature to the labeling game the Soviets are playing with the Krasnoyarsk radar in Siberia.

The ABM Treaty created the Standing Consultative Commission (SCC), which has played an important role to date even though it has been underutilized. We have had excellent people there, including Sid Graybeal, who was our first full-time SCC Chairman. The United States should use the SCC to negotiate agreed statements under, or even amendments to, the ABM Treaty to strengthen the Treaty's basic objectives.

With the ABM Treaty under frontal assault from the President's SDI program, and with the Treaty facing persistent undermining from dual capable systems, we should pause in our examination of START and INF and ask whether negotiations on offensive systems in these or new forums would be possible if there were no ABM Treaty. We must also determine whether that would be possible if the United States abrogated the ABM Treaty, demanded that it be amended to make the SDI program lawful or proceeded forward with the best legal justifications available.

I doubt that it would be feasible to negotiate START and INF treaties if there were not an ABM Treaty. At least that was the premise in the late 1960s when the United States decided we should first negotiate an ABM Treaty. This premise was even more important in the early 1970s when the U.S. insisted at SALT I that negotiations on both offensive and defensive systems had to be undertaken simultaneously. The Scowcroft Commission appears to share this view, particulary in its extensive discussion of arms control in its March 21, 1984 report.

The SDI program reopens the fundamental strategic debate of the late 1960s and early 1970s which was ostensibly closed by ratification of the ABM Treaty. I am not persuaded that emerging technology offers any practical hope for a nationwide defensive system, or that the SDI efforts, if deployed, would enhance security. To the contrary, the pursuit of this dream through "demonstrations" or "tests" and even partial deployment would be destabilizing.

It appears that many members of the current Administration do not share this view of an attempt to build a nationwide defense. They instead favor point defense of fixed ICBM silos. Such an ABM system has a certain logic to it, given the vulnerability of ICBM silos, but it would require amendments to the Treaty. However, a point defense system which included boost, mid-course and terminal phase capability would inherently have nationwide capability. Such a layered system would be at odds with the basic objective of the ABM Treaty.

In conclusion, I am very pessimistic as to the future of arms control over the next five years. The Reagan Administration is not sympathetic to arms control, notwithstanding the Scowcroft Commission report which emphasizes the importance of it. The Administration appears to favor arms control as a tactic to pacify domestic opinion and NATO concerns. Posture and propaganda are the real focus while the United States "rebuilds" its forces over a broad spectrum. The one brilliant diplomatic initiative in search of an agreement--Paul Nitze's "walk in the woods" in July 1982--was rejected by the Administration.

I see little or no prospect for arms control under these conditions over the next five years assuming the President's policies remain essentially the same. Even if, however, the President sought to conclude agreements on offensive systems, and sought to buttress the ABM Treaty, it is not clear that the Soviets have the ability or the will to respond, particularly to entirely new approaches such as "build down" or indexing "destructive potential." We do not know where the Soviets really stand.

Consider, for example, the problem posed by anti-satellite (ASAT) negotiations. At the moment the Soviet ASAT position is a good public posture--a good starting point for negotiations--but their draft treaty includes a prohibition on the use of the Space Shuttle for "military purposes." That was one of the sticking points when the ASAT negotiations began in 1978-1979. It is clearly nonnegotiable.

We do not know, both in terms of their offensive as well as their defensive systems, whether the

Soviets would be prepared to accept significant constraints. As we all know, they have not been very forthcoming on issues dealing with dual capable systems, or with emerging technology and technology change, since the SALT negotiation process began in 1969.

If my pessimism is shared by others, then part of the quest over the next five years must be for actions which stabilize the strategic balance and reduce the risk of nuclear war, but do not necessarily require formal agreement. I see no effort in that direction at present which deals with weapons systems. Negotiations over crisis centers is not enough.

CHAPTER 8

PROSPECTS FOR INF
AND START NEGOTIATIONS

by

Raymond L. Garthoff
Senior Fellow, Brookings Institute

In my judgment, the Intermediate-range Nuclear Force (INF) negotiations are dead, and the Strategic Arms Reduction Talks (START) have no more than a fifty-fifty chance of revival. This is not only a drastically more pessimistic prognosis than that of the Reagan Administration, but also of most critics. Nonetheless, I believe it is valid. Even if INF and START are finished, there does remain both a need and, I believe, a prospect for renewed strategic arms negotiation. Strategic arms limitations, including reductions, would be in the interests of both the United States and the Soviet Union. I believe most leaders of both countries recognize that fact. If this is so, why have we reached the impasse we are now at, and how do we escape it? One answer is that, despite the existence of an objective common interest, we may *not* escape a continuing standoff. And, of course, even if negotiations resume, there is a considerable possibility that agreement would not be reached. But there also remains some possibility that agreement could be reached.

Let us go back to 1980-81 and the origins of INF and START. A new American Administration, unabashedly more skeptical both of arms control and of negotiations with the Soviet Union, entered office. It entered office at a time when American-Soviet relations had already sharply deteriorated, detente had already collapsed, and the one remaining product of seven years of negotiation--the SALT II Treaty--was in danger of failing ratification even before the election of the new administration. While deciding not to seek ratification of either the treaty as signed or its amendment, the Reagan Administration did agree to abide by the constraints outlined in the treaty if the Soviet Union did. It reserved the right, however, to change its mind at any time. Thus, the commitment was conditioned not only upon Soviet performance, but also upon unspecified future considerations.

There remained, however, one other legacy of the past. NATO had taken a decision in December 1979 to pursue a "two-track" approach to long-range theater nuclear forces. The plan was to deploy 572 missiles and also to propose negotiations with the Soviet Union, but to deploy those missiles only if the negotiations did not succeed in reducing the growing Soviet threat in comparable weapons. Further, it was the explicit understanding that the negotiation would be part of the continuing SALT process. The decision itself included a warm endorsement of the SALT II Treaty. Thus, when the United States chose not to ratify the treaty, both tracks of the 1979 decision were in danger of derailment.

The Reagan Administration, and the NATO Alliance, decided to proceed with both tracks because without the attempt to negotiate INF limitations Western European public opinion would not have supported deployment. In the absence of SALT there was no forum for negotiation, so one was created. What previously had been referred to as "long-range theater nuclear forces" (LR TNF) became "intermediate-range nuclear forces" (INF).

Under pressure from NATO governments, who in turn were under rising anti-INF pressure from growing segments of their populations, a decision was made in mid-1981 to propose negotiations. By November 1981 President Reagan announced the NATO position for the INF talks: the so-called zero option. NATO would deploy no United States INF land-based missiles, if the Soviet Union would eliminate its land-based INF missiles. The proposal was an immediate success in its primary purpose. It seized the propaganda high ground and provided political support for continuing INF deployment during the negotiations. It also killed the prospect of any agreement because it was palpably nonnegotiable and because those who preferred deployment to agreement could (and did) prevent the substantial concessions needed to convert the proposal into something conceivably negotiable.

The NATO proposal sought to limit: land-based, intermediate-range missiles, belonging to the United States and USSR, wherever deployed, to zero levels. *Each* of these conditions was heavily slanted to NATO's advantage. The combination was patently nonnegotiable. No one familiar with the situation could expect this proposal to be taken by the Soviet leaders as a serious basis for negotiation, much less for agreement. But this was far from clear to most people.

There were several specific problems with NATO's proposal. First, by seeking to limit constraints on just land-based missiles, not only would the American Poseidon submarine-launched ballistic missiles (SLBMs) be excluded (they could quite reasonably have been omitted because of being covered in SALT), but also the new long-range, strategic submarine-launched cruise missiles (SLCMs). While offering to forego deployment in Europe of the 464 ground-launched cruise missiles (GLCMs), the United States was reserving the right to deploy unlimited numbers of the *same* missile on submarines often in range of the *same* targets in the USSR and Eastern Europe. The initial order in 1981-82 was for 400 such nuclear land-attack strategic SLCMs. It was doubled in 1983.

Second, restricting limitations on INF forces to intermediate-range missiles would have meant excluding all American forward-based systems (FBS). While the Soviets had been prepared in SALT III to limit their own intermediate-range systems, the explicit *quid pro quo* had always included limitations on American FBS aircraft. The Soviets had reluctantly deferred the FBS question during the SALT I and SALT II negotiations, but they have always insisted that the American aircraft were part of the strategic equation.

Third, by restricting proposed constraints to

American and Soviet systems, the British and French nuclear forces (even the small number of French land-based intermediate-range missiles) were excluded and unlimited. Frequently, President Reagan and other American spokesmen have talked about limiting "the two sides" to equal levels--initially, to equal zero levels. Indeed, the 1979 NATO decision talked about equality of the "the two sides." But what are "the two sides?" The adamant U.S.-NATO position has been that only forces of the United States should be included on the Western side. At present, in addition to nuclear capable bombers, Britain and France have 162 missile launchers, all but eighteen of which are on submarines. Both countries also have announced plans for deploying MIRV warheads in profusion. They plan to deploy more than twice as many warheads as the total U.S. INF deployment, and more than the entire Soviet INF deployment to date. So the British and French nuclear forces are not an inconsequential factor.

There are, of course, an array of arguments that can be made as to why the British and French forces should not be counted. The negotiation is (or was) a bilateral U.S.-Soviet one; the French are not part of the integrated NATO military structure; the British and French forces are "strategic" rather than "inter-mediate-range" (even though they are of lesser range than the SS-20); they are sea-based rather than land-based systems; and they cannot substitute for the U.S. deterrent. Of course, the Soviet Union can present a strong case for the necessary inclusion of the British and French forces, but even in terms of NATO considerations the basis for their exclusion from consideration is weak. When we think about strategic planning and the political and military strategy of the Alliance, we absolutely insist on their inclusion. We insist that the Alliance is integral and that an attack on one is an attack on all. Yet, if NATO should be regarded as integral as a target of possible Soviet attack, why should it not also be regarded as integral when considering the nuclear strike forces it marshals to deter such an attack? That is the basis on which the United States expresses its concern over Soviet SS-20s. Why should the Soviet Union dismantle its INF missile forces in exchange for cancellation of a NATO-U.S. deployment program, while a parallel NATO-European missile build-up continues unabated?

Fourth, another condition was "wherever deployed." The Soviet Union has deployed a substantial number of SS-20 intermediate-range missiles in the Far East beyond the range of Western Europe. Yet the U.S.-NATO position in INF was to insist on their dismantlement on grounds of "mobility" and "transportability" of the systems. This is a far-fetched criterion that only points up the much greater ability of the United States to bring other air- and sea-launched systems to bear in Europe.

Finally, the zero level would have meant that NATO would not deploy the 572 U.S. Pershing II and GLCM missiles it proposed to add to existing forces. (They would actually replace only 108 older shorter-range Pershing I missile launchers.) But the Soviet Union would have had to roll back twenty years of strategic history and dismantle not only all of its new SS-20 missiles, but nearly 600 SS-4 and SS-5 missile launchers facing Europe as part of the existing relation of forces since the early 1960s.

In due course, the Western INF position was modified so as not to require zero levels (although even then the changed position was described as "interim" in moving to zero). But none of the other four basic aspects of the proposal were changed.

Ultimately, the outcome of negotiations is decided not by which side is most clever, or most intransigent, in its arguments, but by whether both sides see their interests served by agreement. The Soviets did not, and now that United States INF deployment is proceeding they see no incentive to resume the negotiation.

The Soviet position in INF was also unacceptable to the Reagan Administration and, therefore, to NATO. It would not necessarily have been unacceptable to NATO under other circumstances. Indeed, the final Soviet offer to reduce their INF missiles to far fewer missiles and launchers than existed in the mid-1970s, and even fewer *warheads* than then existed, in exchange for nondeployment of the American INF force could have been regarded as a real victory on the arms control track. The impending U.S. deployment *did* provide bargaining leverage. But in 1983, perhaps unlike 1979, deployment was given a higher value than arms control restraint.

The Soviet and NATO aims in the INF talks were, in the final analysis, incompatible. The Soviets sought zero American INF deployment. In exchange they offered progressively greater concessions in the reduction of their deployments. Ultimately this Soviet proposal might have been considered a fair deal. But it was not so regarded by the United States and other principal NATO governments because their aim was to ensure some (not necessarily the full planned) American deployment. Now the Soviets see no possible value in further INF talks unless the United States and NATO should indeed roll back (or at least soon halt) deployment. They do not really expect that outcome, but it remains the only basis they are prepared to consider. The Soviet walkout was not tactical, but very serious. NATO, in turn, has crossed the politically difficult bridge of beginning deployment. At this point the governments see no gain from negotiating on any basis other than drastic Soviet reductions *plus* Soviet acceptance of some American deployment. In short, there is no basis for an INF agreement, and hence none for resumption of INF talks. INF is dead.

If the Reagan Administration seriously believed the statements of its spokesmen in 1983 and 1984 that the Soviets would only really begin to negotiate on INF once deployment had begun, it was a massive failure to understand the Soviet position. The initiation of deployment marked the end of negotiation, not its beginning, and this was evident long before the deployment began. Similarly, while the United States stands on good propaganda high ground in expressing continuing readiness to resume INF, this policy should not be mistaken for a posture that could lead to the reopening of a negotiation which clearly has ended. Indeed, some Western opponents of an INF agreement are quite satisfied with a situation in which the Russians are to blame for walking out of the INF talks *and* there is no risk of an agreement since the talks are suspended.

I have reviewed the short history of INF first because it was the initial and main negotiation of the early 1980s. The Reagan Administration had preferred to hold off altogether from strategic arms negotiations until it had "restored" American military strength. As noted above, INF talks had soon become necessary because the clock was moving on the two-track NATO decision and opinion in Western Europe would not support deployment if arms limitation talks had not been tried. The Strategic Arms Reduction Talks (START), as SALT was rechristened, in turn became necessary because of unexpected public pressure in the United States.

START, too, was fated to fail. While each side initially took a position "loaded" to its advantage, this could have reflected opening bargaining tactics. The Soviets have, in effect, been attempting to negotiate "SALT III." They have proposed sizable reductions from the SALT II levels. Both sides did make some modifications in their proposals in 1983 moving at least in the direction of possible compromise. In fact, however, there has been no intention on our side to depart from a position requiring deep reductions in Soviet ICBM forces. The aim of reducing drastically Soviet counterforce capability against the United States ICBM force is understandable. But there was no inclination to propose in exchange comparable American sacrifices with regard to the buildup in our own counterforce capabilities. On the contrary, it is often said that only as American strategic military is "restored" (i.e., expanded) will the Soviets have an incentive to negotiate (i.e., to accede to our terms). This American position, particularly in view of the problems created after INF deployment began, meant that the declared U.S. expectation of serious Soviet readiness to negotiate START was at best unrealistic.

Nonetheless, it is still possible to reconsider positions, and to negotiate an eventual compromise START agreement. Now, however, there is first the hurdle of resuming negotiations without either side apparently able to compromise. Moreover, in addition to the difficult intrinsic problems of striking a balance in limitations and reductions that both sides would consider equitable and useful, the weapons on both sides previously addressed in INF remain to be dealt with in some fashion. There also remains the problem of the British and French forces. And now there exists a heavy overlay of mutual suspicion that will make any process of negotiation and compromise even more difficult. Charges of violation of existing arms control agreements pose additional obstacles to negotiation, agreement and ratification.

Finally, the new American Strategic Defense Initiative stemming from President Reagan's "Star Wars" speech of March 1983 has resurrected a whole new dimension to the arms race. It makes attainment of any strategic arms limitation much more difficult. Arguments that this will facilitate offensive arms reductions are either naive or disingenuous.

Ultimately, the prospect for preserving or extending strategic arms limitations and reductions--for START and INF, the expired SALT I Interim Agreement, the unratified but observed SALT II Treaty and the still valid ABM treaty--all depend upon above all the political relationship between the United States and the Soviet Union. And as long as one regards the other as the "Evil Empire," the prospects for agreements to enhance their mutual security seem remote indeed.

CHAPTER 9

ARMS CONTROL
AND THE INF NEGOTIATIONS

by

Robert W. Dean
Deputy Assistant Secretary for Arms Control,
Department of State

Looking back over the past few years it seems clear that the pivotal factor in the arms control dialogue was the issue of United States deployment of large-range Intermediate Nuclear Forces (INF) in Western Europe. Soviet negotiating strategy as well as public diplomacy, in both the INF and START contexts, were designed to prevent these deployments. This strategy reflects--although we do not know this for a fact--a strategic decision taken by the Soviet leadership to do whatever it could to prevent American INF deployment and, in effect, to cashier any chance for achieving agreement on the negotiating front. The Soviets sought to focus the terms of the public debate by first claiming that a nuclear balance existed, then that British and French forces ought legitimately to be included, later that the Pershing II system posed a qualitatively new first- strike threat, and finally that SS-20s deployed east of the Urals posed no threat at all to NATO. This is largely why we now find ourselves where we do. The United States is over the hurdle of initial deployments, and at this point the Soviets must come to grips with the issues which prevent an INF agreement.

There is no more fundamental objective of the United States' negotiating position, in both INF and START, than our insistence on equality of rights and limits between the United States and the Soviet

Union. The Soviets accepted this premise as the basis of agreement in both SALT I and SALT II. Now in START and INF, they are against our position that equal rights and limits for both sides must govern any agreement. Instead, the Soviets protest that equality and equal security must be the indices by which the balance is now to be reckoned. Thus, the Soviets assert the right to maintain INF systems equivalent to all potential nuclear adversaries *combined*, and therefore greater than any one, including the United States. This idea of compensation for non-U.S. nuclear forces is one which no American government has ever accepted. It would mean that if the French, for example, were to increase their national forces by independent sovereign decision, the United States would have to decrease its INF forces in Europe in order to maintain the overall balance.

Moreover, the Soviets claim that a balance of medium-range nuclear forces currently exists in Europe. For this they use a thousand kilometer range limit and include British, French and American forces. Their calculations, I submit, are utterly contrived. In an analysis in 1982 of the theatre nuclear force situation in Europe, which included British and French systems, the prestigious International Institute for Strategic Studies (IISS) in London accorded the Warsaw Pact an overall advantage in arriving warheads of 3.6 to 1. When this calculation is done to include the 400 U.S. SLBM Poseidon warheads assigned to NATO, the Warsaw Pact advantage is still 1.7 to 1. The disparity in overall warhead inventories is even more striking. The Warsaw Pact has 4,000 warheads, while NATO has only 1,600. Now these are not official figures, and as a matter of fact we take issue with the methodology used to draw the calculations. We would argue that the imbalance is even more heavily skewed in the Soviet favor. Also, the IISS figures are dated. They take into account only 325 SS-20s, and today there are over 378. However, they do include the 400 U.S. SLBMs and even British and French systems. I think few would challenge the effort to be objective in the analysis. Even if the figures are subject to some variance, the conclusion is still clear: the Soviet Union maintains an overwhelming advantage. Neither existing British and French warheads, nor the planned deployment of 572 U.S. Pershing II and GLCM warheads, seriously alter that advantage. We must remain clearsighted on this issue and continue to see the existing imbalance for what it is. The Soviet claim that a balance exists is false and disingenuous. It is based on phantom statistics. Furthermore, it obfuscates the real issues along the path to eventual agreement.

The Soviet argument is that British and French forces ought to be included in the balance. Mr. Gromyko has asked rhetorically what difference it makes to the Soviet Union if an attacking warhead is painted with the French tricolor, the British Union Jack or the American stars and stripes. This is a clever but a deceptive way to pose the question. Here again we must recognize that the British and French systems have no place in an agreement which is intended to codify a genuine balance. Given the existing Soviet overall numerical nuclear preponderance, the 162 British and French warheads are nearly irrelevant in any fair calculation of the balance. By any objective standard of balance and equality they should not be an obstacle to achieving agreement. The Soviet Union sought strenuously to include British and French systems during the first phase of both the SALT I and SALT II negotiations. They eventually acknowledged the principle of United States-Soviet equality and dropped the allied systems issue. This would be the proper course when we come back to the negotiating table. The British and French nuclear systems are independent sovereign national forces on which the United States cannot negotiate and for which we will not compensate. They have strategic missions. As a result, they are not comparable to long-range INF missiles which are the subject of the bilateral U.S.-Soviet negotiation.

Finally, and perhaps most importantly, British and French nuclear forces have nothing to do with protecting the Federal Republic of Germany and other nonnuclear NATO states. It would be extremely dangerous to concede the principle that the medium-range balance should be reckoned in terms of Soviet systems on the one side, and American, British and

French systems on the other. For such a principle ignores the roles of United States' systems in protecting Europe, bolstering the U.S. strategic nuclear triad, and thus deterring the Soviet Union. This is really the heart of the matter. It is a point which cannot be repeated often enough. There is a danger in accepting the superficial logic of the Soviet argument. Counting British and French systems is tantamount to decoupling American strategic forces from the defense of Europe.

Another Soviet argument is that the Pershing II IRBMs, the 108 missiles that will be stationed in West Germany, pose a new and special threat because of their short flight time to the Soviet Union. The Soviets assert that they are intended for use as first-strike weapons. The facts are that the fourteen minute flight time of the Pershing II is comparable to the flight time of almost 1,000 Soviet ballistic missile warheads now in position to fire at NATO's European targets. It is also comparable to the flight time of Soviet submarine-launch ballistic missiles which have been positioned off American shores for years. The Pershing II was specifically designed with a range rendering it incapable of reaching Moscow from West Germany. It was included in the original force mix because it was felt that some comparable *ballistic* missile capability had to be deployed against the Soviet SS-20 ballistic missile threat. Also, NATO needs an INF ballistic missile system which will be assured of penetrating the large-scale Soviet defense network which confronts NATO's ground-launched cruise missile (GLCM) force.

How does the Soviet nuclear planner really assess the Pershing II? Does he genuinely believe it poses a disarming first-strike capability? He cannot. One hundred and eight warheads bring within range only a small fraction of the total Soviet land-based ICBM force and an even far smaller fraction of the total Soviet strategic ballistic missile force. Furthermore, only a small portion of the Soviet strategic rocket forces' command-and-control facilities are within range of the Pershing II. All of these Soviet assets, in fact, are targets which can already be covered by the U.S. strategic nuclear force. Thus, the Soviet argument that the Pershing II could be used in a nuclear decapitation strike to eliminate the USSR's ability to coordinate and conduct a nuclear strike of its own is patently false. Such an American capability would require thousands of highly accurate ballistic missile warheads, indeed many more than exist in the entire U.S. strategic arsenal. To argue, as the Soviets have, that the Pershing II gives the United States the capability to conduct a first-strike from Europe is specious. Their sole purpose is to demonstrate to the Soviet Union that should they contemplate aggression against Europe they could not hope to keep it isolated. The new American INF missiles compel the Soviets to assume that an attack on Europe is tantamount to an attack against the United States itself.

PART IV

VERIFICATION AND COMPLIANCE

CHAPTER 10

VERIFICATION AND COMPLIANCE

by

Manfred Eimer
Assistant Director,
Arms Control and Disarmament Agency
Chief, Verification and Intellegence Bureau

In the earlier days of arms control it was believed or hoped that the initial, rather limited steps taken would lead to increasingly more comprehensive agreements. It was also believed that these agreements would be, in a sense, self-enforcing. The agreements would be self-enforcing because there would be strong disincentives against endangering the benefits of arms control by undertaking programs prohibited by agreement. Any such actions would risk detection and could lead to adverse consequences.

However, while the importance of arms control as an element of the U.S.-Soviet relationship grew and the scope and variety of attempted agreements increased, questions relating to verification and compliance were raised whose import have not yet been fully integrated into the arms control process.

There is an irreversible trend towards controlling a greater variety of weapons, many of which are smaller, more mobile and more concealable. The impact on verification of these weapon "improvements" can only in part be compensated for by improvements in the capabilities for collection and analysis of the intelligence data germane to verification. While the growing disparity between systems of interest for limitation and U.S. verification capabilities is troubling, these concerns are overshadowed by the growing realization that arms control agreements have not been self-enforcing.

The President's January 23, 1984 report to Congress concluded that the Soviets have violated, or probably violated, provisions of arms control agreements not only when such violations were militarily significant (or appeared to be the initial steps of militarily important programs), but also when there appeared not to be significant military benefit to the violations. Such Soviet actions tear the fabric of arms control by undermining the political confidence and public support essential for its future.

I

It is difficult to see how, in the future, arms control can play a significant role in the conduct of U.S. national security and foreign policy unless ways can be found to respond to questionable Soviet actions. At a minimum, it must be made clear to the Soviets that they will not be permitted to benefit from treaty violations.

Almost from the inception of the arms control regime, questionable Soviet actions have been referred to by some as "technical" violations or violations of the "spirit" of the agreement (although the "object and purpose" of an agreement is in fact its critical element). Some have tried to explain away concerns by claiming that differences exist between the United States and the Soviet Union in interpretation of the obligations. Such possible differences did not figure significantly in most of the issues analyzed in the President's January 23, 1984 report.

From the point of view of verification and compliance, the most important lesson of the past is that verification needs have not always been given sufficient weight in the drafting of agreement provisions. Moreover, standards of evidence requirements for the purpose of making compliance judgments have often been set too high. Assuring that verification needs are accounted for is a large--but necessary--complication to the drafting and negotiating process. Assuring that questionable Soviet actions are responded to is also a necessary perturbation of the arms control environment. Failing to provide either of these assurances is likely to poison the arms control well.

II

To assure that verification needs are given proper weight in the drafting process, two important assessments need to be made. First, a determination must be made regarding the "degree" to which a prospective accord can be verified; i.e., how easy (or difficult) would it be to circumvent or violate the "object and purpose" and provisions of a prospective accord without being detected? Second, given that assessment, policymakers must assess whether the accord is verifiable enough; i.e., is the accord "effectively" verifiable when other factors (such as military risk, the other party's record on compliance, etc., or, more generally, national security, foreign policy and arms control objectives) are considered in judging whether the agreement in question is in the net interest of the United States?

The first of these phases, that of determining the "degree" to which agreements can be verified, is essentially a technical judgment that attempts to weigh American intelligence capabilities against the systems or activities to be limited. This phase assesses the potential for undetected violations. It must be kept in mind that the only question that should matter to decision-makers is what kinds of violations could *not* be "detected." (The standards of evidence required for "detection" must also be remembered.)

For analytical purposes it must be assumed that before the Soviets would consider carrying out a treaty violation, they would first weigh the benefits from such a violation against the possible negative effect of a "detection." Furthermore, they would assume that a significant violation would, if "detected," result in a significant response. They would, therefore, take all available steps to avoid "detection." While the recent compliance report has shown that violations can be "detected" (in some cases a number of years after the initial strong evidence was obtained), and that the Soviet violation scenarios have not been entirely successful, for purposes of assessing the "degree" to which agreements can be verified it must be assumed that they would carry out violations in such a way that had the most gain for the least risk of "detection."

An early determination of the "degree" to which a particular provision can be verified could suggest how that provision can be redrafted, or what additional intelligence resources should be considered for acquisition to raise the "degree" to which it can be verified.

There can be a large difference in the community of decision-makers about the relative weight given to the various factors that enter the judgment on whether an accord is effectively verifiable. Therefore, it is necessary that the "degree" to which provisions can be verified be described separately from the other factors that go into the effectiveness judgment. The presentation of such separate descriptions to the appropriate committees of the Congress is required by U.S. statute.

The second phase involves a decision by the national leadership, in which the above assessment is only one of several relevant factors to be considered, on whether verification is "effective." Judgments of "degree" of verifiability are properly made by experts in verification intelligence. The final judgment of whether verification is "effective" is properly made by those responsible for directing national policy, both in the Executive branch and the Congress.

III

There should be little question about how the assessment of the "degree" to which provisions can be verified should be made. Nevertheless, for several reasons, including the complexity of formulation, the proper assessments are not always provided or used. What is far from clear, however, is how to balance the military significance of possible provisions with the "degree" to which they can be verified. It is, unfortunately, often true that comprehensive limitations, those which are militarily most meaningful, almost certainly also have components that can be verified to only a very low "degree." Likewise, limitations that can be verified to a high "degree" are likely to be limited in scope. It is fundamentally important that the Soviets take a more constructive attitude toward compliance. If they do, the future of arms control may well depend on how much relative weight is given to the military significance of limitations and to the "degree" to which they can be verified.

CHAPTER 11

VERIFICATION OF
A "NUCLEAR FREEZE"

by

Herbert Scoville, Jr.
President, Arms Control Association

A major initiative to halt the nuclear arms race
proposed by the public sector, as opposed to the
government, has been a "freeze" on nuclear weapons
programs. Specifically, the concept called for a
mutual and verifiable halt on testing, production and
deployment of all new nuclear weapons and the
systems specifically designed to deliver them. The
proposal has been strongly opposed by the Reagan
Administration, and indeed some longtime supporters
of nuclear arms control have been skeptical about the
idea. A major argument used to oppose the freeze
has been that it would be unverifiable, and therefore
would halt U.S. programs while allowing the Soviet
Union to proceed without serious hindrance. This is
not the forum to discuss the overall pros and cons of
a freeze, but I think it is useful to clear up some
misconceptions about its verifiability.

Virtually all arms control measures present some
problems of ensuring compliance and, of course, a
freeze is no exception. However, in my view the
essential elements of a freeze are easier to verify
than most other measures that have been proposed in
recent years. Most of these elements can be verified
to the extent that we could detect on a timely basis
any noncompliance which could significantly effect our
security.

A major factor facilitating the verification of a
freeze is its comprehensive nature. Halting the

testing, production and deployment of a given system, or of the nuclear explosive itself, provides three avenues through which one can obtain evidence of a violation, even though the probability of obtaining such evidence is not equally good for all three phases of a weapons program. For example, our national intelligence ("national technical means" in diplomatic jargon) is by no means as reliable for detecting production of nuclear delivery systems as it is for the detection of testing and deployment. Most of the critically important nuclear weapons systems require extensive testing for development, training, and ensuring reliability. We observe such testing very extensively with our vast array of technical intelligence collection systems, and the legitimacy of using such systems to verify arms control agreements has been agreed to by the Soviet Union. The deployment of any significant number of such systems would have a high probability of being discovered.

Even though the production ban is harder to monitor it should be included in a freeze. If all production were to cease, the verification would be much simpler than if limited production were allowed to continue. In any case even a low probability of detecting secret production would add to the total probability of detecting a clandestine nuclear weapons program.

In sum, a total ban on all aspects of a given weapons program is far easier to verify than would be a partial one which allowed some testing, some production or some deployment. For example, a total ban on cruise missiles would be relatively easy to verify since a single missile or a single test would almost certainly be detected before any significant deployment could occur. On the other hand, a ceiling on cruise missiles, which allowed both sides to have certain numbers or types of these weapons, would be very difficult to verify. It would be hard to count the number accurately and to decide whether cruise missiles for delivery by aircraft were also being used for ground- and sea-launch. There is also the very difficult problem of differentiating between a cruise missile carrying a conventional warhead and one carrying a nuclear explosive. Yet the Administration has included cruise missiles in its START position, and they are also taken into consideration in the so-called "build-down." Presumably the supporters of these measures who are critical of the freeze have some idea of how these problems might be solved since they would not be proposing to the Soviet Union an unverifiable arms control measure. Certainly any solution that works for START would be more than adequate for a freeze. However, it should be pointed out that time is running out in this area. The further the cruise missile programs proceed the harder will be the verification task.

Another factor which makes verification of a freeze relatively easy is the very large stockpiles of fissionable material, nuclear weapons, and nuclear delivery systems that already exist. Therefore, for any violation to be of serious significance, it must occur on a relatively large scale and over a protracted period of time. There is no way in which the Soviet Union by cheating on a freeze could suddenly acquire nuclear superiority.

For example, at the present time the Soviet Union probably has more than 100,000 kilograms of plutonium and even larger amounts of weapons grade U-235. If all production for weapons were halted under a freeze, then it would require a very large secret program over a period of many, many years to add significantly to these existing stockpiles. Since our intelligence was good enough in the 1950s to unravel the Soviet weapons production program when our capabilities were far inferior to that existing today, the chances that a significant clandestine program would escape our detection in a freeze are virtually nil.

With regard to a freeze on testing weapons, procedures for verifying a comprehensive test ban have almost been completely worked out with the Soviet Union in negotiations which ended in 1979. The Soviets have agreed to the concept of having unmanned seismic stations in the Soviet Union and to the concept of invitational inspections for ambiguous events which cannot be resolved in a Consultative Commission.

The difficult verification area for a freeze is the

same one which exists for all other arms control measures; that is, how to deal with dual capable systems. The definition of what should and what should not be included could be extremely difficult. This is more of a treaty negotiating problem than a verification one. There will always be difficulties of deciding on what exactly should be included in a freeze or in any other arms control agreement, such as the INF negotiations.

Fortunately, those weapons which are the most dangerous and need to be frozen at the earliest time are ones for which this problem is not a critical factor. For example, counter-silo ballistic missiles which can threaten the deterrent of the other side are easily distinguishable from conventional weapons. Procedures for verifying these have already been worked out in the SALT negotiations. These are the systems that need to be dealt with first; then some of the more peripheral problems can be tackled in later discussions. In some cases it might not be practical to include these at all. But there is no question that verification of a freeze on the most dangerous nuclear delivery systems, and on the nuclear weapons themselves, can be adequately verified so that our security will not be threatened.

CHAPTER 12

COMPLIANCE DIPLOMACY

by

Michael Krepon
Senior Associate,
Carnegie Endowment for International Peace

I

Compliance problems will arise under the best of circumstances. No arms control agreement can be written to cover every future contingency. In many instances, agreements will be purposely vague because both sides may not wish to foreclose military options or because they cannot reach a mutually agreeable limitation.

If relations between treaty signatories are in reasonably good shape and if parties to an agreement wish to maintain its viability, compliance issues can be ironed out in mutually satisfactory ways. If, on the other hand, relations between treaty signatories begin to deteriorate, and if one or both parties to an agreement start to question its immediate worth or its long-term viability, compliance problems will not be resolved satisfactorily. In such a political environment current negotiations will stall and previous agreements will begin to unravel.

As the need to stop the process of unravelling becomes increasingly apparent, it also becomes increasingly difficult as each side has less of an incentive to be forthcoming on individual cases. On the contrary, both sides seek to protect themselves against a further unravelling of the agreements by defining treaty obligations in more permissive ways or by exploiting ambiguities in treaty texts. Some will characterize these activities as violations; others will see them as prudent hedges. Either way, they have a cumulative political impact. Political relations between the treaty partners continue to sour and the checks against this unravelling process are weakened. In the current political environment, imagine a meeting of the National Security Council or the Defense Council in the USSR: who at either table would argue not to hedge bets against current arms control agreements for fear of undermining them further?

In response to the current crop of compliance problems, many have called for improved monitoring capabilities and more precise treaty provisions for any future arms control agreement. Both are important, but neither can ensure treaty compliance.

Improvements in national technical means (NTM) of verification may encourage American presidents to enter into agreements they might otherwise avoid and to generate support for those agreements by wider segments of the Congress and the public. But no matter how much U.S. monitoring capabilities are improved, they do not prevent problems from arising when signatories define their treaty obligations in unhelpful ways. Detecting such troubling activities has not been the problem in the past. The problem lies in defining an appropriate response.

More intrusive verification provisions will not necessarily help on treaty compliance questions. On-site inspection can be a useful tool at times--such as when destroying stockpiles or verifying a comprehensive test ban treaty--but it is hardly a cure-all for treaty compliance. On-site inspections, like improvements in NTM, can provide somewhat greater assurance of compliance. Nevertheless, a system of inspections can provide high confidence against cheating only for the short time before, during and after the inspection takes place.

Precise treaty language can also promote treaty compliance. Other concerns over Soviet compliance can be alleviated by avoiding difficult-to-verify provisions that generate more problems than they solve such as the SALT II provision governing new ICBM types. Even with precisely drafted agreements, possibilities for circumvention will continue to exist, especially when U.S.-Soviet relations begin to slide.

When compliance problems arise, U.S.-Soviet relations must be on track in order to sort them out. Compliance diplomacy cannot succeed when U.S.-Soviet relations have deteriorated to the point where one or both sides perceive a lack of interest in maintaining the viability of existing agreements. Unless both sides believe these agreements have a future, the accords will continue to unravel.

In theory, a president with Ronald Reagan's hardline anti-communist credentials has more leeway to stop this process of decontrol than presidents of a more liberal orientation because he has greater freedom to maneuver on U.S.-Soviet relations. Likewise, conservative presidents can defuse concerns over treaty verification and compliance by appealing for public trust in their judgment that the United States can monitor Soviet compliance and respond effectively to Soviet misbehavior. By large majorities, the electorate and the Congress will also be inclined to trust Ronald Reagan's judgment that previous compliance problems should not stand in the way of new agreements. Irreconcilables in the Congress will bitterly contest these findings, but they can be isolated effectively with an erstwhile ally in the White House.

Ever since Ronald Reagan was elected this hopeful scenario has sustained those who want the President's pragmatism to prevail over his ideology. After all, "ideologues" in the Kremlin have long since demonstrated an ability to deal with hardliners in the White House when it was in their interest to do so. Ronald Reagan, however, has not been an activist president with respect to negotiations, and no nuclear arms control agreement has been reached without the active intervention of an incumbent president. Reagan has yet to demonstrate either a substantive grasp of the issues under negotiation or a sense of priorities and trade-offs needed to achieve them. Nor does he have a strong and experienced figure to assist him in either the Cabinet or the White House. These deficiencies have been blurred by the absence of effective leadership in Moscow and by the rigidity of Soviet negotiating positions. Even with key changes in personnel in the Reagan Administration, it is unclear that progress can be made in negotiations. But without such changes, it is difficult to see how President Reagan can make headway in arms control negotiations or in compliance diplomacy.

Any president to the left of Ronald Reagan faces an entirely different set of problems on verification and compliance issues. The more such a president is inclined to take risks for arms control benefits, the more vulnerable he will be in the political arena, particularly if he is perceived as lax in pursuing strategic modernization programs or unsteady in his handling of U.S.-Soviet relations.

Arms control oriented presidents will be especially sensitive to news leaks of compliance problems when they are characterized as violations by those most opposed to arms control agreements. For reasons discussed earlier, these issues will continue to arise regardless of how carefully drafted new agreements are. Some compliance questions will be of little consequence, others may be quite substantive in nature.

As a result of previous controversies, it is no longer sufficient for a president--regardless of his political orientation--to say these allegations have no merit or that they are being addressed in quiet diplomatic exchanges. A positive strategy for dealing with compliance issues is needed which clearly lays out for the electorate as well as for the Kremlin the steps an administration plans to take when questions arise.

Effective compliance diplomacy is predicated on the recognition that existing agreements remain in the interests of both sides to uphold. This is no less true today than when the SALT process began fifteen years ago. Those most desirous of doing away with the 1972 Anti-Ballistic Missile (ABM) Treaty might ask themselves how they intend to reorient United States strategy and deployments toward defensive systems if Soviet offensive deployments are unconstrained by existing agreements. Who would benefit from the demise of the ABM Treaty? How would either side be better off if the launcher ceilings incorporated in the SALT I Interim Agreement and SALT II Treaty went by the boards? Any realistic analysis of the current and foreseeable strategic environment leads to the conclusion that the object of intelligent U.S. diplomacy should be to shore up arms control agreements reached under Presidents Nixon, Ford and Carter.

At this point, the most effective signal to indicate a commitment to continued SALT compliance would be a presidential announcement of our readiness to extend the ceilings on offensive forces established in the Interim Agreement and SALT II Treaty. Official intentions toward the ABM Treaty present a more difficult problem, given the scope of current Soviet activities and President Reagan's Star Wars initiative. But Soviet activities do not begin to provide the Kremlin with an effective capability to defend the USSR against nuclear attack. Likewise, Star Wars research activities are a long-term proposition which will proceed in the face of daunting technical challenges and limited resources. Both sides are well aware of these constraints, and they provide a strong military rationale for maintaining the ABM Treaty in place.

II

The components of an effective compliance strategy can be inferred from the definitions of "adequate" verification used by every president from John F. Kennedy to Jimmy Carter. These presidents did not assert they could detect every instance of Soviet noncompliance with agreements negotiated under their auspices. They did, however, assert they could detect Soviet cheating of any consequence, and in time to take appropriate countermeasures. By implication, the United States should first try to achieve a satisfactory explanation or solution to compliance concerns through diplomatic channels before moving when necessary to countermeasures if diplomatic channels fail.

With the downturn in U.S.-Soviet relations and increased concerns over treaty compliance, it would be wise to make this common sense, two-track strategy explicit. For SALT related issues, the diplomatic track should start with the Standing Consultative Commission (SCC), where there are procedures and precedents to deal with compliance problems in mutually acceptable ways. Other diplomatic channels should be used sparingly because the SCC is best suited to resolve problems that arise. Nevertheless, it may be necessary to reinforce or facilitate the work of the SCC by higher level diplomatic exchanges. While the diplomatic track is being used, it makes little sense to issue public reports or presidential findings of noncompliance since "going public" will only make satisfactory solutions in private harder to achieve.

If compliance diplomacy does not yield a satisfactory solution, offsetting actions may be required. If this second track is needed, countermeasures should be proportional to Soviet activities and within treaty constraints whenever possible. The purpose of U.S. countermeasures is to convey our willingness to maintain the viability of current agreements and to emphasize our determination to take effective action when the viability of an arms control regime is challenged.

A positive two-track compliance strategy will place American presidents in a better position to respond to the substantive and political problems arising from Soviet compliance questions. The approach suggested here will not alter the opinions of those who automatically assume violations have taken place, but it will help assure the political center that compliance questions are being addressed in a purposeful and sequential way. The details for implementing such a strategy cannot be spelled out in advance. Specific responses will depend on individual cases and presidents must have flexibility to handle compliance problems when they arise.

In some instances, military responses and countermeasures to evidence of noncompliance may not be wise or appropriate. Few would argue that the United States should, for example, resume development and production of biological warfare agents as a result of evidence that the Soviet Union is not living up to its obligations under the 1972 Biological Weapons Convention and the 1925 Geneva

Protocol. A conclusive explanation for "yellow rain" may never be available. In the interim the most appropriate response to new reports of "yellow rain" may again be public presentations of the evidence, since private attempts to stop these practices or to elicit from the Soviet Union and Vietnam alternative explanations for these phenomena have not been successful so far. Early resort to public diplomacy makes sense when there are reports of casualties, when private bilateral exchanges are unsatisfactory or when the arms control agreements governing these practices have no consultative or compliance provisions.

For nuclear arms control compliance questions public diplomacy should be the course of last resort, unless the activity in question poses serious security problems that mandate quick action. Diplomatic channels tend to work slowly, especially when complex treaty provisions and military practices are involved. Still, the time consumed in the SCC will be only a small fraction of that involved in awaiting the deployment of new nuclear weapon systems.

If, after the course of extended efforts at the SCC, the United States receives no satisfactory explanation for Soviet activities, public reports explaining U.S. diplomatic efforts, Soviet responses, and the rationale behind American countermeasures are essential. For example, if the United States is concerned about Soviet compliance with the ABM Treaty, a president could act to deploy defensive systems of our own or to improve the penetration capability of our offensive nuclear forces. The choice of military countermeasures, when needed, requires considerable skill since what appears proportional to one side may appear disproportionate to the other. The countermeasures must also be chosen wisely to secure congressional and public support, and to elicit an appropriate response from the Kremlin. On the latter point, the Kremlin's reading of an administration's intentions is critical, as is the political context in which countermeasures are adopted.

In the above-mentioned case, the intent of the American response should be to uphold the viability of the ABM Treaty, not to accelerate its demise. Arms control oriented presidents are in the best position to convey this signal when carefully proportional military countermeasures are adopted. In the example above, the most appropriate American response would be to improve the penetration capabilities of our offensive nuclear forces. A president committed to the ABM Treaty also has the option of deploying a defensive countermeasure without necessarily implying a lack of commitment to the treaty regime. The same action chosen by an administration deeply skeptical of the ABM Treaty would likely convey the entirely different message of preparing to withdraw from treaty constraints.

Compliance problems jeopardize new agreements as well as those already in force. These political dynamics can be defused somewhat if new arms control agreements contain consultative provisions and procedures to handle prospective compliance problems. In addition, future presidents may find it necessary to endorse safeguards against prospective compliance problems. Like the use of proportional countermeasures in ongoing disputes, the purposes of safeguards are twofold: to encourage strict Soviet compliance and to assure the American public that U.S. interests will be protected in the event of troubling Soviet behavior.

The concept of safeguards is not new. Presidents Kennedy and Nixon readily accepted them when proposed by skeptics of the Limited Test Ban and SALT I accords. Future presidents would be wise to initiate this process early in negotiations rather than after their conclusion. Establishing criteria for safeguards early on can help minimize the substantive and political risks of entering into an agreement--but only if safeguards are chosen wisely.

For example, an ASAT agreement clearly poses risks if the Kremlin fails to comply, although these risks seem less ominous than the risks of an unfettered competition in anti-satellite warfare. To deal with "breakout" scenarios or covert Soviet cheating against ASAT provisions, there are several alternative safeguards to shorten the timeline of an appropriate U.S. response. These possibilities include allowing a certain number of ASAT tests prior to an agreement, restricting tests in ways that limit operational capabilities, or, best of all, banning flight tests altogether and establishing a production line which can be opened in the event the Soviets resume ASAT tests.

As in the case of proportional countermeasures, there is no substitute for choosing reasonable safeguards. If an administration believes the risks of entering into an ASAT or any other arms control agreement are inordinately large, the preferred safeguards are likely to be so excessive as to foreclose the possibilities of an accord or to minimize its value. An arms control oriented president is not likely to share this calculus of benefits and risks. For him, the selection of prudent safeguards can make a difference in the record of Soviet compliance and in the outcome of ratification debates.

It should be evident from this discussion that compliance diplomacy is at least as difficult and critical as the process of negotiating arms control agreements with the Soviet Union. To be successful at both, future presidents will need considerable skill along with much imagination and common sense. These traits are still not sufficient for presidents of a moderate-to-liberal bent. They can propose well-reasoned and artful strategies to deal with verification and compliance problems and still find themselves in political hot water. Unlike conservative presidents, they will not be in a position to defuse easily these controversies. Arms control oriented presidents must assume the unalterable opposition of the political right. Their success will depend on convincing the political center that the benefits of agreements negotiated under their auspices are worth their attendant risks. Presidents with reputations for vacillation or weakness are unlikely to succeed in convincing the electorate to take these risks, particularly during periods of disturbing Soviet activities in areas unrelated to arms control agreements.

The composition and orientation of the Senate is not as hostile to arms control as it was during the SALT II debate. Events in the interim have naturally led to second thoughts, with more Senators inclined to play constructive, supportive roles in future debates. Nevertheless, approximately one-fifth of the Senate is likely to oppose future agreements executed by anyone but a conservative president--the same proportion of Senators who opposed the Limited Test Ban Treaty in 1963.

Unlike conservative presidents, moderates cannot expect to sway these votes. It would be a mistake for them to try to do so both at the outset of negotiations and after their conclusion. The most effective way to outweigh concerns over verification and compliance is to bring home agreements that will generate widespread and enthusiastic public support. If the benefits of agreements are strongly appreciated, verification and compliance risks will not weigh heavily in public debate. This was the case during the Limited Test Ban Treaty. If public support is not forthcoming, these issues will resonate strongly, as was the case during the SALT II debate. Future agreements do not need to yield immediate, significant results to meet this criterion, but they must promise steady, progressive benefits over time. Otherwise, future presidents most inclined to reach arms control agreements with the Kremlin may find themselves unable to secure the necessary votes in the Congress.

PART V

CONFIDENCE-BUILDING AND RISK REDUCTION MEASURES

CHAPTER 13

UNMANNED ON-SITE ICBM LAUNCH MONITORING

by

Victor A. Utgoff[*]
Deputy Director, Strategy and Force Division
Institute for Defense Analysis

My paper presents a new idea for reducing the probability of accidental nuclear war. The kind of nuclear war I have in mind is one which grows out of a crisis as a result of the Soviet Union or the United States receiving a false indication that the other side has launched its international ballistic missiles (ICBMs).

I

While the probability of such an accident is extremely low, current trends in the strategic balance may be working to increase it. In particular, improving accuracies of new Soviet ICBMs are making our ICBMs more vulnerable to attack while they are still deployed in their silos. Our ICBMs force is improving too, of course, and by the late 1980s both sides' ICBMs will be vulnerable to rapid missile attacks by the other side.

These growing vulnerabilities in both sides' ICBM forces are creating an increasingly dangerous context for interpreting false attack warning signals, particularly during deep crises. In such crises, both sides will be extremely nervous about the possibility that the other may conclude that war is inevitable. The opponent may thus elect to make a preemptive strike against the other side's ICBMs in hopes of destroying them before they can be launched. A false attack warning signal in a deep crisis may thus tend to be confirmed by its receivers' worst fears.

While I would expect attack indications to be examined carefully, the pressures of the moment could conceivably lead to a hasty decision to shoot back. The likelihood of such an unfortunate string of events is very low, but the costs of such an "accident" would be enormous.

II

These observations suggest that we should seriously consider additional measures for reducing the probability of getting such false attack warnings--particularly if relatively inexpensive means can be found.

This raises an interesting question: why not agree with the Soviet Union to monitor each others' ICBM fields with on-site unmanned ICBM launch detectors?

III

For our side, the net effect of installing such a monitoring system would be to raise the number of independent launch detection systems from two to three. In addition, an on-site monitoring system would detect potential missile launches from a very different vantage point. It would observe portions of the potential flight trajectories of Soviet ICBMs from distances of no more than tens of miles. In contrast, our early warning radars and early warning satellites must detect ICBMs from thousands and many thousands of miles, respectively.

An on-site warning system would also allow cross-checking between two independent sensor systems within two minutes. The current attack warning system does not guarantee independent cross-checks of missile attack indications from the satellite warning system until sufficient time has elapsed for the missiles to rise above the horizons of early warning radars located in North America.

The effects for the Soviet Union of installing a system of ICBM launch detectors in the United States should be generally similar.

III

The Defense Nuclear Agency funded a proposal by the Institute for Defense Analyses to examine the technical feasibility of this idea. This paper summarizes the main results of that feasibility study.

1. The record of our arms control negotiations was examined to see what it could tell us about how the Soviet Union might react to a proposal to implement an on-site unmanned ICBM launch monitoring system.

2. The functions, characteristics and costs of the monitoring system derived are described.

3. The implications for European interests of pursuing this idea are assessed.

4. The potential collateral values of implementing such a system are summarized.

These collateral values are a major reason for considering the implementation of this concept.

IV

Our examination of the arms control record yielded a number of significant conclusions.

First, it suggests that the Soviet Union has had a serious and continuing interest in the general problem of accidental nuclear war. This is reflected in their participation in the Surprise Attack Conference held in Geneva in 1958; the Hot Line Agreements (further improvements in this area are even now being negotiated); and the agreement on Measures to Reduce the Risks of Outbreak of Nuclear War. These various actions do not provide a basis for concluding the

Soviets have been so concerned about the possibilities of nuclear war as to accept intrusive or burdensome measures to reduce it, however. The burdens associated with the agreements I have mentioned have been quite low. Further, in the course of the Surprise Attack Conference, the Soviet Union explicitly rejected a suggestion that teams of foreign observers be stationed near their missile launch sites to verify that these missiles had not been launched.

Nonetheless, the Soviet Union has apparently seen some arms control agreements as worth significant intrusion. They agreed to local installation of foreign sensors for monitoring peaceful nuclear explosions above a certain aggregate yield. This agreement would be more significant if the Soviet Union had ever declared that it would be carrying out such explosions and had allowed the agreed measures to be implemented. In the course of negotiating toward a comprehensive nuclear test ban (CTB) treaty, the Soviet Union also agreed in principle to emplacement of ten unmanned sensor stations on their territory. Again, this agreement would be more significant if the CTB Treaty had been completed and its provisions had been implemented.

The arms control record also shows that the Soviet Union was the first nation to suggest using unmanned on-site sensors. It did this in the course of negotiations toward a nuclear comprehensive test ban treaty back in the early 1960s.

V

The arms control record makes clear that the Soviet Union would insist that information collected by any foreign sensor systems located on Soviet territory would not go beyond the minimum required to meet the objective of the agreement the sensors' systems were intended to support. The Soviet Union gave ground very grudgingly when negotiating the CBT Treaty, the provisions allowing on-site monitoring of large peaceful nuclear explosions, and the agreements not to interfere with national technical means employed to monitor the provisions of the SALT II agreement. The Soviet Union clearly considers its superior ability to keep its internal activities secret a major advantage over the West.

Finally, the provisions agreed to as part of the agreement on peaceful nuclear explosions, and in the course of negotiations on the CTB Treaty during the late 1970s, make it clear that the Soviet Union will insist on every possible precaution to ensure that they understand perfectly the nature and function of any unmanned sensors located on their territory. In order to do this, they will insist on a record of all information returned to the United States along with the codes needed to decipher any encrypted information in this record. Similarly, the Soviet Union will insist on receiving exact copies of any equipment installed on their territory. This equipment will be completely dismantled and tested to ensure that all its functions are completely understood.

VI

Keeping this information from the arms control record in mind, we derived the following monitoring system.

After examining a number of sensor types, we chose a microwave radar. This sensor type appears to be the best choice when cost, reliability, technology transfer constraints, degree of obtrusiveness and maturity of the technology are taken into account.

Our system would employ radar stations located roughly 50 to 60 kilometers down-range toward the operator's country. These radars would look straight upwards through the minimum volume of space encompassing all feasible launch trajectories from the ICBM field being monitored and toward the operator's country.

The radar station monitoring each ICBM field in the host country would be continuously linked to a control station in the operating country by means of commercial communications satellites. These communications links would be used to report instantaneously any detected launches. They would also be employed to report tampering with the operating country's monitoring equipment.

To fulfill their purpose the stations must have a high probability of detecting missile launches, particularly when launched in large numbers. As designed, the radar stations would have a probability of one in a hundred of failing to detect a launch of a single missile. The stations would have a probability of one in a billion of failing to detect the launch of an attack of five or more missiles.

The radar stations must have a low false alarm rate and an extremely low false alarm rate for large attacks. As designed, the system of radar stations we would need for monitoring the Soviet Union's ICBM fields would collectively generate a false alarm of a single launch on the average of once every six months. More important, the stations would generate a false alarm of a simultaneous attack launched from at least two separate ICBM deployment areas less frequently on average than once every 10,000 years.

These probabilities of detection and false alarm rates compare favorably with those that have been reported for our other missile attack warning systems. They strike us as more than adequate, but could be raised further without significantly increasing the costs of this kind of monitoring system.

To fulfill its purpose our system of monitors must be safeguarded against covert tampering. The potential approaches to covert tampering can be divided into three kinds.

First, attempts could conceivably be made to tamper covertly with the internal workings of the monitors. To prevent this we would have to agree that approaching the station would be prohibited, except in the company of authorized representatives of the operating country. To monitor compliance with this agreement, the stations would each be fenced and instrumented to detect approaches. The main instrument for this purpose would be a sensitive seismometer located in a deep well dug beneath each station. The readouts of the seismometer would be continuously communicated to the operator's country.

Second, attempts could conceivably be made to block covertly the view that the radars are supposed to maintain the volume of space they are to monitor.

To prevent this the radars are designed with sufficient sensitivity to detect any conceivable surface that might be employed to block their view. As a second safeguard against this approach to tampering, we employ a system of four check satellites in low altitude polar orbits. Each check satellite carries on a conversation with each radar station as it passes overhead. The radar stations report the results of each conversation when it happens; the check satellites report when they next pass over their operator's country. With this system of four satellites every radar station would be checked every three hours.

Third, attempts could conceivably be made to substitute covertly counterfeit communications for those generated by the monitoring system. To guard against this encryption, devices are employed to append to each block of communicated information some authentication bits. Upon receipt of each block of information, the operating country would employ a copy of the authentication device to regenerate the authentication bits and check them against those that had been appended to the information at its source.

To satisfy the Soviet Union's requirement that it be able to decode any encrypted information, it would also be given copies of the encryption device. It would not be given the information needed to key correctly the encryption device until the devices in service with the radar monitoring system had been through several cycles of code changes.

These various safeguarding techniques should adequately protect radar monitoring systems from covert tampering. To maintain high confidence in this monitoring system it would seem appropriate to maintain continuously a "red team" effort to study and test ways to subvert it.

Finally, we should note that providing samples of these radar monitors to the Soviet Union would not constitute a transfer of technology that could be used to increase the military threat posed to us. All components employed would either incorporate the national seismic systems the U.S. government planned to provide to the Soviet Union in implementing a comprehensive nuclear test ban treaty or incorporate technology that we know the Soviets have already.

VII

The costs to the United States for supplementing a monitoring system of this kind were estimated in some detail. To get the system built, installed and operating would cost approximately $55 million in 1983 dollars. Thereafter, it should cost approximately $10 million in 1983 dollars each year to keep the system operating. This implies a ten-year total cost of approximately $155 million, which is a very small fraction of the costs the U.S. will pay during the 1980s for its other missile attack warning systems.

In calculating our cost estimates we included every significant cost we could imagine, from fees paid to the Soviet government for transporting the stations to their deployment sites to the writing of manuals for the technicians that would maintain them. The annual costs include substantial allowances for replacement components, estimates of the tariffs for use of the communications satellites, and sufficient travel and per diem to cover one week-long maintenance visit to each station by a four-man team every six months. The individual components were estimated by adjusting the costs of analogous components that have already been built.

Given the level of detail of our estimates, and the fact that all components are essentially off-the-shelf, we believe our estimated total ten-year system cost would prove accurate to 30% in real terms. The cost to the Soviet Union for an analogous system to monitor our ICBM deployment fields would be somewhat lower because the United States has fewer missile fields.

VIII

Our examination of the possible implications for our European allies of negotiating and implementing a cooperative on-site ICBM monitoring system of the type described above suggests they would favor such an effort.

Our European allies seem even more sensitive to the risks of accidental nuclear war than we are. They see themselves as very likely to be involved in any nuclear war between the superpowers. At the same time. they see themselves as having little direct control over the initiation and prosecution of such a war.

Our allies are not likely to see this monitoring system as exerting much influence on the degree to which their defense is coupled to the U.S. strategic forces.

Our allies might see an effort to negotiate and implement an agreement to install this kind of monitoring system as diverting attention from more important arms control efforts. On the other hand, they may feel that the superpowers have more than enough capacity to undertake this additional arms control effort.

Pursuing this concept with the Soviets might also highlight fear on the part of our European allies about the possibility of accidental nuclear war. Alternatively, the Europeans may already be more than adequately aware of the possibilities, and simply applaud this effort to improve the situation.

IX

The potential collateral benefits derived from negotiating and implementing this kind of on-site ICBM launch monitoring system seem large in the aggregate.

Given the way the monitors had to be designed, there is little prospect for gaining intelligence information beyond that which the monitoring system must produce to meet its objective of detecting ICBM launches. Some information might be gained from detections of launches of missiles for testing and training purposes. It might even be necessary to install temporarily one of the monitoring stations within a missile test range to test the monitoring system's performance.

In addition, the instrumentation employed to guard

against unauthorized approaches to the monitoring stations may pick up conversations, other interesting sounds, heavy equipment movement and perhaps some additional data on underground nuclear tests. The host country can easily minimize the amount and value of such information, however.

By accepting such a system on its territory each country would provide improved warning of an intended ICBM attack on the other. Improved short-term warning would be provided if the monitors were left operating. If they were shut off for any reason, their owner would thus receive a longer-term warning that foul play may occur. A country that does not intend to ever attempt a surprise attack on the other would therefore benefit from installation of such monitoring systems on both sides.

Perhaps the most important collateral benefits that might be derived from the negotiation and implementation of a monitoring agreement of this kind is the valuable precedent that would be set in legitimizing a new kind of information gathering process for arms control purposes. While on several occasions the United States and the Soviet Union have agreed in principle to the installation of the other's unmanned sensor systems on its territory, monitoring procedures of this kind have never been carried out.

Finally, the experience gained in negotiating and implementing a monitoring agreement of this kind may clarify the feasibility and value of other forms of unmanned on-site monitoring.

X

In summary, our overall conclusions show that:

1. a cooperative missile launch monitoring system to reduce the probability that a false attack warning would lead to accidental war seems to be technically feasible;

2. $65 million ($55M + $10M) per year could create a reliable, minimally intrusive and independent detection system;

3.   valuable precedents for arms control would be set in the process;

4.   our European allies seem likely to support the idea;

5.   the Soviet Union would probably find it difficult to refuse to consider this idea, but might impede negotiations on it pending progress elsewhere.

Finally, we should note again that this monitoring system is obviously not a complete answer to the question of accidental nuclear war. It addresses a fairly specific potential cause of such a war. Moreover, its value is likely to drop as time passes. By the 1990s both sides may have sufficiently large numbers of mobile strategic missiles to destroy any fixed ICBM system deployed by the other. In this case, each side's ICBM launch monitoring system would provide a safeguard against *one* rather than *all* sources of possible false alarms of preemptive attack against its silo-based ICBM force. Even further in the future, both sides may abandon the concept of silo-based deployments of ICBMs. When this day comes the system proposed here will cease to have any significant purpose. Until that day comes, however, the unmanned launch monitoring system described above would have significant value, particularly when its collateral values are also taken into account.

AUTHOR'S NOTE

*The author is indebted to the Institute for Defense Analyses (IDA) and the Defense Nuclear Agency(DNA) for their permission to draw on material prepared by IDA for DNA. The author is grateful to his colleagues at IDA who performed much of the technical work upon which this article is based, and to many others who provided helpful suggestions, but most of all to the late Mr. Joseph Beardwood, III, without

113

whom this work would not have been done. The author bears sole responsibility, however, for this interpretation of this work.

CHAPTER 14

BEYOND THE HOTLINE: CONTROLLING A NUCLEAR CRISIS (A SYNOPSIS)*

by

William L. Ury
Program on Negotiation, Harvard Law School
and Richard Smoke
Consultant to the Program on Negotiation,
Harvard Law School

Perhaps the most likely path to nuclear war today is through a crisis that escalates out of control because of miscalculation, miscommunication or accident. President Reagan highlighted this danger in a speech in Berlin in June 1982, and again drew attention to it in his January 16, 1984 speech on U.S.-Soviet relations. Our strategic defense efforts have focused on deterring the Soviets from launching a deliberate attack. In part because of the success of these efforts, the chief danger now is not war by cool calculation, but war by runaway escalation.

With the dangers of nuclear terrorism, nuclear proliferation, and trouble spots all over the world, the possible scenarios for an unintended war are gradually multiplying. The United States and Soviet Union could be drawn into a regional war in which each had vital interests, such as in the Middle East, Korea or Europe. A "mad" leader armed with a few atomic bombs, believing that his nation or terrorist group would be better off without the superpowers, might detonate a bomb in an American city hoping thereby to trigger a Soviet-American exchange. A missile might be fired by accident or without authorization. Perhaps most dangerous is the scenario no one foresees.

There is thus a rising need for effective crisis control. One of the most serious threats in a crisis is each side's capacity to make wise decisions under pressure. Improving that capacity is the task of crisis control. It deserves special attention in its own right, complementary to efforts at arms reductions.

An analysis of past U.S.-Soviet crisis behavior beginning with the Cuban Missile Crisis highlights the critical factors which can skew even the most rational decision-making under pressure and suggests measures which each side can take in advance--separately and jointly--to prevent or control a crisis.

Four key features of a crisis make it especially dangerous: little time to decide, high stakes, high uncertainty, and few usable options. These factors press decision-makers to take hasty, often escalatory, action to protect vital interest. Through action and reaction, miscalculation and miscommunication, a runaway crisis and war may result.

This suggests taking steps in advance to ensure that in a crisis situation: 1) there is adequate time for each side to make a wise decision, 2) the stakes are kept under control, 3) dangerous uncertainty is reduced, and 4) each side is left acceptable ways out of the crisis.

A "stabilization strategy" in time of crisis addresses the core dilemma of how to defuse a dangerous crisis while protecting vital national interests. It involves blocking or freezing offensive military action so as to deny the other side any gains by arms and simultaneously initiating immediate negotiations to protect both sides' essential interests in security and national credibility. In terms of the four crisis factors, blocking military action helps gain time for decision-making and reduce the perceived stakes, while negotiation helps reduce dangerous uncertainty and expand the options available for a peaceful resolution. These steps require preparatory measures in advance, which ideally would head off crises even before they start.

A stabilization strategy has in the past proved successful even in some difficult instances where one side, presumably assessing the risk of nuclear war as acceptably low, has sought unilateral gain by military action. Khrushchev's sending missiles to Cuba in 1962 is a case in point. Kennedy's skillful combination of military blocking action--the naval "quarantine"--and high-level personal communication and negotiation succeeded in defusing the crisis while protecting vital national interests.

In some instances it may be possible to block the other side without counterescalating in a way that threatens its security. Land mines and tank barriers along borders, the interposition of third forces, and other defensive techniques might reduce the risk to one's own vital national interests without increasing the risk to those on the other side. Developing additional techniques of this kind is a promising area for military research and development.

Six specific measures which could help stabilize or, even better, prevent a crisis with the Soviet Union are suggested for consideration. They are not guarantees against crises, but rather small practical steps that can reduce the risk. Building on present crisis mechanisms like the Hotline and current proposals to improve it, the United States and USSR could, in effect, construct a "crisis control system."

Each proposal of course has its risks and limitations, which need to be carefully weighed against its benefits. For instance, unless considerable care were taken, a crisis control center might be misused by the Soviet Union for intelligence gathering or disinformation. Furthermore, unless the diplomatic groundwork were laid, the proposal might be misperceived by our allies and by China as evidence of superpower collusion. Clearly, the measures should depend not on goodwill or trust, but solely on the self-interest that the United States and the USSR share in avoiding unintended war.

AGREED-UPON CRISIS PROCEDURES: A set of technical procedures which the United States and the USSR would carry out before or during crises to

defuse unintended crisis triggers.

The Hotline was established to give the American and Soviet heads of government a way to communicate quickly in a nuclear crisis. In 1972 the two sides reached an "Incidents at Sea" agreement. It created a rule book for their respective navies to avoid potentially dangerous incidents and provided for regular joint meetings to review how well the rules were working. Such agreed-upon procedures make it technically possible both to prevent potential crises and to cope more effectively with any that do occur. These essentially nonpolitical procedures are in both sides' interest and should function even in times of tension.

Successful crisis procedures created to date provide a basis for developing additional ones. To prevent crises, the United States might consider proposing further "incidents agreements" for accidental ground and air intrusions (like that of Korean Airlines Flight 007) as well as limited but regular consultations on proliferation and the possibility of nuclear terrorism.

To contain crises, the superpowers could adopt such measures as procedures for coping with nuclear detonations whose source and motive are unclear; procedures to signal peaceful intent in time of heightened expectation of war (here termed "Hands Off Holsters" signals); prearranged procedures to facilitate face-to-face negotiations in times of crisis; and enlargement of the existing crisis codes for instant and accurate Hotline communications. For halting inadvertently triggered incipient hostilities, the United States might consider a discussion of contingency procedures for a cease-fire and return to *status quo ante* as well as an East-West communications channel for commanders in Europe.

The essential value of these agreed-upon crisis procedures lies in making sure that when the leaders of each side want to avoid or defuse a crisis, they will not fail for simple lack of the machinery to do so.

NUCLEAR CRISIS CONTROL CENTER: Joint U.S.-

Soviet facilities in Washington and Moscow, connected by instant teleconferencing, at which diplomats and military officers would continuously monitor potential crises to help prevent inadvertent war.

If a nuclear bomb suddenly were to detonate in San Francisco, American suspicions would naturally fasten on the Soviet Union. But the bomb might have been exploded by a third nation, a terrorist group or through a Soviet accident. In such a case American leaders would want proof, and the Soviets would surely want to cooperate. No one would want to go to war over a mistaken assumption.

The Hotline--even an "enhanced" one--might be inadequate for the delicate tasks of interpreting and authenticating information. It might be valuable for the leaders of both countries in such a situation to have available a group of highly trained military and diplomatic experts from both sides who already knew each other and had prepared together for just such a crisis.

In advance of a crisis the joint professional working group could anticipate potential crisis triggers and develop technical procedures like those just described for handling them. The center's officers, moreover, might serve as a support staff to ongoing Cabinet-level talks with the USSR on crisis prevention and control (described below), thus helping to ensure the center's relevance to policymakers' concerns and to increase the likelihood of its expertise being tapped in time of crisis.

The concept of such a center has attracted considerable attention, most recently in a bipartisan report issued by Senators Sam Nunn and John Warner.

As mentioned earlier, unless handled with considerable care a crisis control center could potentially involve certain problems, including disinformation at critical moments, intelligence leaks, added bureaucracy and foreign perceptions of U.S.-Soviet condominium. The center therefore should not be oversold. It might best be implemented in increments, perhaps beginning with a bilateral standing commission. The commission at first might have a narrow mandate, derived perhaps from the 1971 "Accidents Measures" Agreement, to develop measures to prevent and control crises arising inadvertently, such as from accidents, nuclear war in the Third World or nuclear terrorism.

CRISIS CONSULTATION PERIOD: A declaratory policy, agreed-upon or unilateral, of reflection and consultation following one (or a few) nuclear detonation(s) on one's territory in order to ascertain its origin and the intentions behind it before making a retaliatory strike.

The strenuous American efforts to prevent an accidental or unauthorized U.S. launch do not forestall the possibility of such a launch from the USSR (or in the future from another nuclear power). Should one or a few warheads detonate within the United States, pressures on high-level American decision-makers would be immense, especially if civilian casualties were large. Anticipating a rapid and large-scale U.S. retaliation, the Soviet Union might follow up the unintended strike with a rapid and deliberate, or perhaps even full-scale, attack.

An agreement to consult could shift expectations, reduce fears that all-out war was imminent, halt immediate military action, and buy time for decision-makers to think through an extraordinarily difficult and confused situation. An agreement to consult would reinforce the norm that in nuclear emergencies the most significant action possible is for the two governments to talk.

Such an agreement (or unilateral policy as suggested by Robert McNamara) has a certain trade-off: it somewhat reduces the other side's uncertainty about immediate retaliation for a very small deliberate strike in return for a margin of safety in avoiding accidental war. It seems worthwhile in part because the probability that either nation would launch such a small strike without expecting eventual retaliation in kind seems much lower than the chance of an unintended detonation. And indeed the United States and the USSR have already agreed implicitly to such a policy in the 1971 "Accidents Measures" Agreement and the 1973 Prevention of Nuclear War Agreement.

This measure would make the policy explicit.

NUCLEAR RISK REDUCTION TALKS: Semiannual meetings between the U.S. Secretaries of State and Defense and their Soviet counterparts to discuss measures to prevent and control crises.

None of the agreed-upon procedures and ideas for a center can come into being without negotiation between high-level policymakers on each side. Agreement, if it comes, is likely to be in incremental steps. Moreover, as new potential dangers arise, new measures will be required. All this suggests the need not for one-shot negotiations, but for ongoing regular talks.

Some agreements, because of their delicacy and susceptibility to misinterpretation by others, would remain necessarily informal. Indeed, useful discussion would likely revolve not just around possible agreements, but around basic assumptions and the intentions of each side so as to reduce the chance of miscalculation and misunderstanding. Because of the informal nature of these exchanges, they might best take place between those who would later be centrally involved in the crisis decision-making process, such as the American Secretaries of State and Defense and their Soviet counterparts. Should a crisis occur, officials already would have a working relationship with their opposite numbers--a wish frequently expressed by American participants in past crises.

Such talks carry, of course, a certain risk of misunderstandings and false confidence. While this calls for considerable caution in the talks, it probably does not outweigh their potential benefits.

In short, regular semiannual Cabinet-level talks on crisis prevention and control would serve to create and maintain an ongoing "crisis control system."

PRESIDENTIAL CRISIS CONTROL SEMINAR: A briefing and "crisis exercise" for the president (or president-elect) and top advisers in which specialists and participants in past crises would pass on their

accumulated learning.

While the president receives some preparation for fighting a war and using nuclear weapons, apparently little preparation is provided for defusing a nuclear crisis safely and successfully. Yet decisions in a nuclear crisis would likely be the most important decisions a president would ever make. Controlling such a nuclear crisis, moreover, is like launching a mission to the moon: an extremely complex system must work perfectly the first time.

A given president will likely make real "hands-on" crisis decisions only once, if ever; no practice is possible. But it is possible to transfer to a new president and a new staff the accumulated wisdom and experience of past nuclear crises in the form of an intensive briefing over several days. Participants in those past crises, most of whom are still alive, could discuss the lessons they learned, assisted by experts in military affairs, history and international relations. The president and staff members might also observe or participate in one or more simulations of an emerging crisis in order to explore the difficulties of keeping a crisis under control.

ENHANCED THIRD-PARTY ROLES IN DEFUSING REGIONAL CONFLICTS: Superpower support for third-party activities in situations where regional conflicts could draw the superpowers into an unwanted and dangerous confrontation.

Perhaps the most likely source of superpower confrontation is a regional crisis in the Third World which draws in the superpowers. Regional mediation before the United States and USSR become directly involved may be the most effective means of forestalling escalation. While there is a long history of third-party efforts, their effectiveness could be enhanced.

Potential third parties include the United Nations, neutral countries, and regional organizations like the OAU or OAS. One of the most successful efforts in recent years was the British mediation of the

Zimbabwe/Rhodesia conflict, which threatened to escalate. Measures which might assist such efforts are the greater use of regional congresses called in time of crisis to head off superpower entry; the development of an international mediation service comprising distinguished senior mediators and a trained staff; and the creation of a "rapid-deployment" international peacekeeping force. Political, financial and logistical support from the United States and the USSR for third-party efforts could often make the crucial difference between failure and success.

The time seems right for a major initiative for nuclear crisis control. These six measures, together with the Hotline and other existing procedures, would help to form a "crisis control system." Progress in crisis control seems especially feasible. It is clearly in each side's interest to eliminate the danger of unintended war. Moreover, the measures for doing so do not appear to provoke the same fears of military inferiority as do arms reductions. Because the danger of runaway crisis is growing more salient and because much can feasibly be done to control it, crisis control offers one of the most significant opportunities today to reduce the risk of nuclear war.

AUTHOR'S NOTE

*This synopsis summarizes the key findings of a report done for the U.S. Arms Control and Disarmament Agency in April 1984 entitled, *Beyond the Hotline: Controlling a Nuclear Crisis.* The authors are grateful to ACDA for its generous support of this research. The views expressed here are those of the authors and do not necessarily coincide with those of ACDA or any other agency of the United States government. The report and further information may be obtained from the Nuclear Project, Harvard Law School, Cambridge, MA 02138.

CHAPTER 15

CONFIDENCE BUILDING AND RISK REDUCTION MEASURES

by

Dean Sackett
Commodore, U.S. Navy
Assistant Deputy Director for International
Negotiations, Office of the Joint Chiefs of Staff

While new weapons technology and arms control efforts can, as we have learned, contribute to strategic stability, the threat of nuclear confrontation will most likely be with us as long as the ideological differences between the superpowers remain. But there is a very real difference between the *threat* of nuclear war and the *risk* of outbreak of nuclear war.

The threat, which we must respect, is with us because the nuclear arsenals and ideological differences exist, but the risk of nuclear attack can be lessened. Risk can be reduced by establishing in peacetime means of communicating during crises and by agreeing to measures intended to reduce the possibility of accidental confrontation or miscalculation. In this regard, those confidence building agreements currently in being provide the basis for considering additional measures.

Contribution to Stability

Confidence building measures are designed to enhance mutual knowledge and understanding about military forces and activities. The overall objective is to reduce the likelihood of an accidental confrontation, miscalculation or failure of communication; to inhibit opportunities for surprise attack; and to enhance stability in times of calm or crisis.

Confidence building measures cannot be expected by themselves to redress imbalances in military power-- that is a job that encompasses more than just the arms control dimension. But confidence building measures can enhance stability, if they can achieve one or more of the following objectives:

1. Reduce uncertainty about the size, structure and activities of a potential adversary's military forces;

2. impede shows of force or other acts of military intimidation during periods of tension;

3. enhance warning by providing indications of actions which may have hostile or threatening appearance.

Achievement of these objectives depends on both the willingness to engage in negotiations aimed at establishing suitable measures and subsequent compliance with agreed measures. Our experience in these endeavors is modestly encouraging.

Agreements in Force

United States and Soviet efforts to reduce the possibility of nuclear confrontation date from the 1950s, but it took the 1962 Cuban Missile Crisis to propel the two governments into establishing the first agreement on the subject--the so-called Hotline Agreement of 1963.

The Hotline Agreement established a direct communications link between Washington and Moscow consisting of two terminal points with teletype equipment, a full-time duplex wire telegraph circuit (Washington-London-Copenhagen-Stockholm-Helsinki-Moscow), and a full-time duplex radiotelegraph circuit (Washington-Tangier-Moscow). The communications link has proved its worth over the past 21 years, most notably during the Arab-Israeli wars of 1967 and

1973. In 1971, recognizing the positive experience gained from operating the Hotline, the two parties agreed to improve the link by installing two satellite communications circuits.

The institution of the Hotline was but a technical means of communicating regarding developing crises. What was more important was to recognize the need to manage or reduce the risk that a crisis or accident would bring about nuclear war. Hence, in the course of the Strategic Arms Limitation Talks (SALT I), the United States and the USSR negotiated and signed in 1971 the Agreement on Measures to Reduce the Risk of Outbreak of Nuclear War. The "Accident Measures" Agreement requires each side to guard against accidental or unauthorized use of nuclear weapons, to notify the other in advance of planned missile launches in the direction of the other party, to notify the other of an accident or unexplained incident involving a possible detonation, and in the event of any unexplained nuclear incident to reduce the possibility of its actions being misinterpreted by the other party.

The Incidents at Sea Agreement, signed in 1972, enjoins the United States and Soviet Union to observe strictly the letter and spirit of the International Regulations for Preventing Collisions at Sea, to refrain from provocative acts at sea that could increase the risk of war, and to notify mariners of actions on the high seas that represent a danger to navigation or to aircraft in flight.

Again in the context of the SALT I negotiations, an agreement on prevention of nuclear war was signed in 1973. This accord requires the two sides to refrain from acts that could exacerbate relations, or lead to nuclear war between them or between one of them and another country. It also recognizes that each party must refrain from the threat or use of force against the other party and to consult in the event of heightened risk of nuclear war.

In addition to these bilateral accords, the United States is a party to the 1975 Helsinki Final Act of the Conference on Security and Cooperation in Europe (CSCE), which contains confidence building measures applicable to the participating states. These primarily involve prior notification of military maneuvers and are designed to reduce the risk of war through miscalculation of other states' intentions. Such measures are most appropriate in Europe where there exists the greatest concentration of military forces in the world.

New Initiatives

These existing agreements have contributed to reducing the risk of nuclear war, but there is certainly room for improvement. Hence, in 1982, President Reagan proposed a new series of bilateral confidence building measures to be negotiated in the INF and START talks. These confidence building measures would provide for expanded exchange of information on each side's forces, and for advance notification of major military exercises and of all ballistic missile launches. To demonstrate American seriousness and goodwill, we voluntarily notified the USSR of plans for the major military exercise GLOBAL SHIELD in 1982, 1983, and again in 1984.

In the Department of Defense Authorization Act 1983, the Congress directed the Secretary of Defense to conduct a full and complete study and evaluation of possible initiatives for improving the containment and control of the use of nuclear weapons, particularly during a crisis. That study, which involved all concerned U.S. government agencies, was completed in April 1983. The Secretary of Defense transmitted the study results in his April 1983 *Report to the Congress on Direct Communications Links and Other Measures to Enhance Stability.*

That report recommended three measures to improve the direct communications network between the United States and the Soviet Union:

1. The addition of a high-speed facsimile capability to the Hotline;

2. a parallel Joint Military Communications Link to allow exchange of highly technical information on a rapid basis. Such a link could be

used in urgent consultations on terrorist nuclear activity;

3.   improvements in diplomatic communications facilities in our respective embassies to reinforce the capabilities of the two ambassadors to act as the personal representatives of the head of state in both times of crises and calm.

The latest round of communications improvement talks took place in Moscow in April 1984. The talks have marked significant progress only in the first of the U.S. proposals dealing with the Hotline. Regrettably, the Soviets have thus far been reluctant to pursue the other two.

On the European front, the Conference on Disarmament in Europe, known as the CDE, began in Stockholm in January 1984. It is an outgrowth of the CSCE process and has a mandate to develop confidence and security building measures which go beyond the Helsinki Final Act. In January, NATO allies tabled a package of measures which contain much more stringent notification and information measures as well as mandatory observation and verification provisions. Specifically, the measures called for:

1.   Information exchange on ground and air forces in the CDE zone;

2.   forecasts and notifications of military activities in the zone, including amphibious operations, mobilizations, and alert activities, as well as regular out-of-garrison activities;

3.   mandatory invitations to observers at these activities;

4.   the right of on-site inspection by challenge;

5.   facilities for improved communication between participants.

It remains to be seen whether the Warsaw Pact states

intend to negotiate seriously on these proposals.

The Soviet Approach to Confidence Building Measures

The Soviet Union has expressed support in principle for progress in confidence building measures both in the CSCE context and in START. However, Western negotiating experience suggests that the Soviets have a different view of these measures from that of the West. The Soviet concept in many cases emphasizes voluntary expressions of goodwill rather than concrete contributions to enhanced stability. Frequently, Soviet proposals have involved declaratory devices, such as non-first-use of nuclear weapons, which would add nothing to European security or to commitments already undertaken in the U.N. Charter or the Helsinki Final Act. In other instances in which the Soviets have advanced proposals which would restrict specific military activities, the measures have been vaguely defined or designed to inhibit U.S. and allied military flexibility critical to maintaining an effective deterrent, while leaving Soviet forces and activities relatively unaffected.

Conclusion

Confidence building and risk reduction measures can be helpful as part of this nation's efforts to achieve greater international security and stability. Additional measures are worth pursuing, but they must be addressed prudently in a building block fashion so that expanded cooperation can grow out of the foundation that has been laid. As noted at the beginning, we must live with the threat of nuclear confrontation. However, we can, with cooperation from our adversaries and allies, make every effort to reduce the risks of that confrontation from ever occurring.

CHAPTER 16

CONFIDENCE-BUILDING MEASURES

by

Richard F. Staar
Senior Fellow, Hoover Institution on
War, Revolution and Peace

In and of themselves confidence-building measures (CBMs) do not reduce either armed forces or weapons. However, they can contribute to greater stability and security. CBMs are designed to inhibit miscalculations, failures in communications and opportunities for a surprise attack.

The United States and the Soviet Union have entered into several understandings that involve confidence-building measures. The 1963 Hotline Agreement established a direct link between Washington, D.C. and Moscow; the 1971 "Accident Measures" Agreement was signed to prevent an accidental nuclear war; and the 1972 Incidents at Sea Agreement prohibits acts at sea that could increase the risk of war.

Helsinki Conference

The Conference on Security and Cooperation in Europe (CSCE) adopted several confidence-building measures in its Final Act, which was agreed to by 35 heads of government on 1 August 1975 at Helsinki. They included:

1.   Obligatory notification of major military maneuvers involving more than 25,000 troops;

2.   voluntary notification of maneuvers on a smaller unspecified scale (NATO policy is to announce those in the 10,000 to 25,000 range);

3.   voluntary exchange of observers at maneuvers;

4.   voluntary notification of major military movements.

Before 1981 the USSR met the above requirements in a minimal manner. During August of that year, intended perhaps as a threat to invade Poland, the Soviet Union announced maneuvers in the Baltic and Byelorussian military district as well as on the Baltic Sea. Neither the number of troops nor the name of the exercise were revealed as required by the CSCE Final Act. Only after Western protests did *TASS* report that "Zapad-81" included approximately 100,000 men.

The Vienna Talks

The Mutual and Balanced Force Reductions (MBFR) negotiations in Vienna also have dealt with confidence-building measures under the general term "associated measures." In 1979, the twelve NATO delegations proposed a package as follows:

1.   Each side would notify the other in advance of out-of-garrison activity by one or more division-size formations. The sole exception was that alert activities need be announced only at the time when they begin.

2.   The right to send observers to prior notified out-of-garrison activities would be guaranteed to both sides. (The West proposed also that measures (1) and (2) cover the territory of all European participants in the Vienna talks, not just the reduction area, and that they should include a considerable part of the western USSR.)

3.   Major military movements by ground forces of those direct participants, whose home territory is outside the reduction area, into the area of reductions would also require prior notification.

4.   Each side would have the right to conduct an annual quota of inspections on the territory of the other side in the area of reductions. Inspection teams would conduct their surveys from the ground or air, or both.

5.   Permanent exit/entry points would be established to monitor military movements into and out of the area. Observers would be stationed at these points for the duration of the treaty.

6.   Information would be exchanged on forces to be withdrawn. There would be periodic exchanges of information on personnel strength and organization of forces in the reduction area.

7.   Interference with national technical means of verification, meaning photography from reconnaissance satellites, would be prohibited.

All of the foregoing confidence-building measures were written into the draft treaty submitted by NATO representatives in July 1982 to the Warsaw Pact delegations. In addition, the West indicated that participants would consider establishment of a consultative mechanism to oversee implementation of the provisions in the agreement. If the U.S.-Soviet Standing Consultative Commission (SCC), established in 1972 to monitor adherence to SALT I, were to become the model, meetings would be held only twice a year. (The USSR in 1983 turned down an American request for a special session of the SCC.)

The Warsaw Pact's views are close to those of the West on certain elements of the package. There is a basic disagreement, however, on some fundamental aspects of NATO's associated measures proposal. Areas of disagreement include: (1) the proposed geographic extension of the first two measures, which involve prior notification of out-of-garrison activities by one or more division-size units and the presence of observers at these notified activities, beyond the reduction area into the European part of the USSR; (2) existence of exit/entry points for the duration of the treaty; and (3) on-site inspection.

The need for what are known as cooperative means of verification has been repeatedly emphasized to the Soviet Union at the highest levels. The late USSR President Brezhnev indicated in an interview with the West German magazine *Der Spiegel* (2 November 1981, p. 58) that "if confidence is reciprocally achieved, then also other forms of verification can be developed." However, he expressed the thought that national technical means were sufficient. No concrete evidence of a change in the Soviet attitude on this question has occurred as of this writing. *Pravda* on 3 May 1984 carried an article by military commentator Yuri Lebedev, who stated that the USSR would not accept stricter verification procedures in future East-West arms control agreements. He rejected American proposals for on-site inspection.

Negotiations at Stockholm

The Conference on Confidence and Security-Building Measures and Disarmament in Europe (CDE) originated in May 1978, when President Giscard of France proposed that such a gathering discuss CBMs first and later take up disarmament issues in a potential second stage. The United States insisted that the following criteria be met as a prerequisite for holding such a conference. The confidence-building measures discussed had to be militarily significant, verifiable, politically binding, and applicable to the whole of Europe from the Atlantic to the Urals. The U.S. also refused to consider any naval or air confidence-building measures that were not an integral part of a notifiable ground activity. President Reagan endorsed the French proposal in February 1981 as long as it was based on the above criteria. The United States also deferred any commitment to actual force reductions during a second stage of the CDE conference.

The Political Committee of NATO developed a package of CBMs as a basis for the Western position at the CDE talks in Stockholm. A U.S. Department of State official outlined on January 14, 1984 the six points of the proposal:

1. Annual exchange of information on ground and air force units. Information would include unit designation, headquarters location, and composition down to brigade, regiment or wing levels. This measure would increase transparency and complement Western exercise notification proposals. The formulation avoids overlap with the MBFR talks concerning exchange of information on personnel strengths.

2. Notification of major military activities. The proposed time period is extended to 45 days in advance of the exercise. The threshold for reporting regular out-of-garrison activities would be lowered to 6,000 men. Mobilization, including reservist call-up, of 25,000 troops would be notifiable as would alert activities upon initiation. Amphibious landings in the CDE zone by one brigade, or 3,000 men, also would be notifiable. NATO also proposed an exchange of forecasts about the above activities for one year in advance in order to create a political obstacle to the use of exercises with a coercive or signaling intent.

3. Verification. The proposal would include a clause legitimizing and prohibiting interference with national technical means of verification. It would cover all 35 countries represented at Stockholm. The proposal would use the principles already contained in Article XII of the 1972 United States-USSR Anti-Ballistic Missile Treaty.

4. There would be an obligation to invite

observers from all interested participating states at all notified activities, including alert activities, after a specified interval. Treatment of observers and information provided them must be agreed upon. The CBM value of this provision is modest due to its potentially guided-tour nature and the dispersal of ground force activities.

5.   On-site Inspections. Each CSCE government would be permitted one inspection per year, with a possible limit on the total number any state is forced to accept. The area should be specified and inspectors accompanied by their hosts. The United States had proposed inspection either by air or from the ground.

6.   Consultation and communication. Communication might be crisis-oriented, with each CSCE member designating competent authorities for bilateral contacts to resolve emergencies. Another approach envisages establishment of a dedicated telex system to circulate routine CDE traffic. Creation of a consultative commission to address matters of compliance and clarification also has been suggested.

When comparing the confidence-building measures proposed by the West in 1984 at Stockholm during the CDE conference with those in the NATO draft treaty submitted almost two years earlier in the MBFR negotiations, it is apparent that considerable overlap exists. The latter included prior notification and observers at out-of-garrison activities, prior notification of certain movements, a fixed annual quota of ground and aerial inspections, declared entry and exit points for military personnel, exchange of information on manpower and force structure, noninterference with national technical means, and a consultative commission.

When the CDE convened on January 17, 1984 in Stockholm, U.S. Secretary of State George Shultz addressed the opening session. He expressed the hope to build on what had been achieved in Helsinki and elsewhere. Specifically, he said:

> We should look for ways to make surprise attack more difficult; to make miscalculation less likely; to inhibit the use of military might for intimidation or coercion; to put greater predictability into peaceful military exercises, in order to highlight any departures that could threaten the peace; and to enhance our ability to defuse incipient crises. Our aim, to use the current phrase, is to increase the transparency of military activity in Europe.

Instead of responding positively to Shultz's remarks, *Pravda* on February 8, 1984 selected one phrase as follows: "The United States does not recognize the legitimacy of the artificially imposed division of Europe." *Pravda* misinterpreted this statement to mean that the United States supports a revision of territorial boundaries in Central Europe. Instead, Secretary Shultz was speaking about human rights and implementation of the Helsinki process "through practical steps to break down barriers, expand human contact and intellectual interchange, increase openness, and stretch the boundaries of the human spirit."

On the second day, Andrei A. Gromyko addressed the CDE delegations at Stockholm. In contrast to Secretary Shultz, the Soviet foreign minister accused the United States of being "the main threat to peace"; of exporting "militarism, enmity and war hysteria" to Europe; and of responsibility for the breakdown of arms control talks. Gromyko finally did mention that his government would be willing to discuss early notification of troop movements and military maneuvers. However, the USSR would propose (1) a NATO-Warsaw Pact nonaggression pact, (2) a treaty on no first-use of nuclear weapons, (3) reductions in defense budgets, (4) a ban on chemical weapons, and (5) a nuclear-free zone in Northern Europe. These ideas were presented at the CDE, although a detailed proposal was not submitted by the USSR until May 8, 1984. A book published the preceding year in Moscow listed all of these proposals as acceptable (O.N. Bykov, pp. 70-72).

Western and most neutral country delegations looked upon the Soviet proposal for a new agreement on the renunciation of force as representing a duplication of what had been agreed to already in the United Nations Charter and the Helsinki Final Act. In order for such an old formulation to acquire new meaning the Soviet Union would have to agree to nonaggression against other Warsaw Pact members as well as NATO and the neutrals.

Western reaction to the second concept, namely a no first-use of nuclear weapons treaty, was negative and viewed as propaganda. If signed, it would preserve the East's advantage in conventional armed forces throughout Central Europe. Should this overwhelming superiority ever be used the West must reserve the option of launching nuclear strikes in order to stop the invasion. Only an MBFR agreement and then actual reduction of troops to equal levels can lead to a treaty on no first-use. Unfortunately, the Warsaw Pact refuses to admit that it has conventional superiority.

The problem with the third Soviet proposal, a freeze on defense budgets, is that the USSR has never revealed its true military expenditures. For example, under "Ministry of Medium Machine Building" are hidden outlays for nuclear weapons procurement. Many other items are similarly shrouded in secrecy. The Stockholm International Peace Research Institute's *The Arms Race and Arms Control 1983* (New York: Taylor and Francis, Inc., 1983, p. 149), laments the fact that its own analysis depends "so little on material coming from the Soviet Union itself." Thus, it would be impossible to ascertain whether a defense budget has been frozen or reduced when no outsider is permitted to know the facts.

The fourth Soviet proposal, a ban on chemical weapons in Europe, has been discussed for several years at the U.N. Conference on Disarmament (CD) at Geneva, and as of today it is still being talked about. Indeed, Vice President Bush offered an American draft treaty on April 18, 1984. The main obstacle remains the USSR's refusal to permit on-site inspection, although Ambassador Viktor L. Israelyan did suggest that such a provision might be acceptable. Furthermore, a treaty limited to Europe would not prevent chemical weapons from being stored east of the Ural mountains. It is estimated that the Soviet Union has built its stockpile to some 350,000 tons over the past fourteen years.

The last proposal for a nuclear-free zone is not new. Its origins date back to the 1957 Rapacki Plan for Central Europe. Other areas have included the Baltic Sea (Walter Ulbricht), the Balkans (Todor Zhivkov), the Mediterranean, and most recently Northern Europe (supported by Sweden). Apart from not complying with the CDE mandate that agreements encompass the whole of Europe, there is always the possibility of moving nuclear weapons expeditiously into a geographically restricted zone from the outside. In addition, only the USSR has nuclear weapons in Northern Europe. They are stockpiled adjacent to Norway and Sweden, and are carried on submarines as well. On the other hand, none of the Scandinavian governments will permit stationing of nuclear weapons on its territory. This prohibition includes NATO member states.

The only separate proposal from an East European delegation came from Romania. It offered details, rather than the Soviet Union's general declaratory statements, on prior notification of military maneuvers and troop movements. However, the figures appear to be much higher than those proposed by the West. It has been reported also that the Romanian proposal includes little on verification procedures. It does provide details on advance exchange of information prior to major military movements. Interestingly enough, Oleg A. Grinevsky, the head of the Soviet delegation to CDE, at a news conference during the last week of January 1984, brushed aside a question about that part of the Romanian proposal.

Finally, the eleven neutral European countries at the CDE conference took a long time to agree on a joint approach in Stockholm. Most of the disagreement centered around three points, according to *Dagens Nyheter* (March 1, 1984, p. 16):

1. Sweden proposed that the paper contain a reference to its own doctrine of "joint securi-

ty." Switzerland took a negative stance because of its policy of deterrence, which holds that a potential aggressor should be forced to pay a high "admission fee" when invading Swiss territory. Other neutral delegations supported the Swiss.

2. Yugoslavia put forward a proposal to reduce military forces in "certain border zones" along the frontiers of neutral and nonaligned states. Again the Swiss opposed this for their own territory, even though the area might not be wider than 50 kilometers. Sweden also appeared to be cool to the idea.

3. Yugoslavia views a NATO-Warsaw Pact non-aggession agreement as contributing to a better international climate. Sweden and Switzerland make reference to the principle of nonaggression in their working papers. Opinions were divided on how best to express the foregoing in the neutral nations' *demarche*.

Some compromises were reached, and a document was submitted on March 8, 1984 by only eight of the neutral delegations. It called for more detailed exchange of information on military movements that could lead to a statement on renunciation of force. If the neutral nations' proposals are accepted, "they thereby create conditions for considering a reaffirmation, in appropriate ways and forms, of the commitment to the peaceful settlement of disputes, undertaken in the United Nations Charter and the Final Act" (*New York Times*, March 23, 1984).

The first CDE round lasted from January 17 through March 16, 1984, and the next one was convened in early May. Apart from the press conference mentioned earlier, the USSR delegation head also addressed the Union of Sweden-Soviet Societies in Stockholm. He stated that American Pershing II and cruise missiles in Europe had increased military as well as political tensions. However, the Soviet Union did not regard the present international situation as irreversible. That is why the USSR and other Warsaw Pact countries were concentrating on large-scale initiatives. Their implementation would "restore trust in Europe as a whole" (Moscow radio, TASS in English, 1 March 1984; *Foreign Broadcast Information Service* - International Affairs, pp. CC 4-5, March 1, 1984.)

Future Prospects

Conclusions are premature because the CDE talks may continue until November 1986 when the next CSCE follow-on conference opens in Vienna. However, it does seem that the Soviet Union to date has used the meetings in Stockholm as a propaganda forum. Even the Stockholm statement by Secretary Shultz was taken out of context and distorted with the obvious intention of playing on West European fears. Unrelated issues have been brought up repeatedly by the USSR. The deployment of Pershing II and ground-launched cruise missiles was often mentioned. The Soviets also took the opportunity to blame the United States for the breakdown of the talks in Geneva, when it was they who walked out. None of these issues pertains to confidence-building measures. This is why the West has refrained from bringing up the SS-20 problem as well as the most recent Soviet introduction of SS-21, SS-22 and SS-23 theater nuclear missiles into Central Europe.

Although the neutral nations have been slow in orchestrating their position, it is obvious that they intend to play the role of broker between East and West. This had been done rather successfully at the Madrid follow-on conference to the Helsinki Final Act. Conciliation, of course, signifies compromise. The problem here is that consensus means unanimity. Hence, there is the danger that an agreement may not be reached in Stockholm except on the least meaningful measures in the confidence-building field.

Bibliography

1. Alford, Jonathan, "Confidence-Building Measures in Europe: The Military Aspects," *Adelphi Papers*, no. 149 (London, spring 1979), pp. 4-13.

2. Birnbaum, Karl E., ed., *Confidence Building and East-West Relations* (Vienna: Wilhelm Braumueller, March 1983), pp. 132. 79

3. Bykov, O. N., *Mery doveriya* [Confidence-Building] (Moscow: Nauka, 1983), pp 7.

4. Gromyko, Andrei A., "Address at Stockholm Conference," *Pravda* (19 January 1984), p. 4.

5. Larrabee, Stephen, and Dietrich Stobe, eds., Confidence-Building Measures in Europe (New York: Institute for East-West Security Studies, 1984), pp. 221.

6. Mutz, Reinhard, ed., *Die Wiener Verhandlungen ueber Truppenreduzierungen in Mitteleuropa* (Baden-Baden: Nomos Verlag, 1983), especially pp. 297-303 for text of NATO draft treaty.

7. Petrovskii, V. F., *Sovetskaya kontseptsiia razoruzheniia* [Soviet Approach to Disarmament] (Moscow: Nauka, 1983), p. 76.

8. Sanakoev, Sh., "Road to Confidence and Security in Europe," *Mezhdunarodnaya zhian'*, no. 3 (1984), pp. 21-32.

9. Shultz, George, "Building Confidence and Security in Europe," *Current Policy*, no. 538 (Washington, D.C., January 17, 1984), p. 3.

10. Staar, Richard F., ed., *Arms Control: Myth versus Reality* (Stanford, Calif.: Hoover Institution Press, 1984), especially Chapter 4,

"The MBFR Process and Its Prospects" by R. F. Staar on pp. 47-56 and "Discussion" by Harriet Fast Scott on pp. 96-100.

11. Stockholm International Peace Research Institute, *The Arms Race and Arms Control 1983* (New York, Taylor and Francis, Inc., 1983), p. 254.

12. Report of the Secretary-General, Reduction of Military Budgets (New York: U.N. Department for Disarmament Affairs, 1983), p. 99.

13. U.S. Congress, Commission on Security and Cooperation in Europe, *CSCE Digest* (Washington, D.C., November 1983-April 1984).

14. U.S. Department of State, "Arms Control: Confidence-Building Measures," Gist (Washington, D.C., January 1984), p. 2.

15. _____, *Implementation of Helsinki Final Act* (Washington, D.C., 1984), Special Report No. 113, p. 35.

Table 1

Verification Categorization

Regimes	Methods	Systems
1. Absolute verification	1. General on-site inspection	1. Photo-recon-aissance satellite
2. Adequate verification	2. Selective on-site inspection	2. "Ferret" satellite
3. Limited verification	3. Challenge on-site inspection	3. Nuclear-radiation detection satellite
4. Token verification	4. Control posts/ observer/liaison missions	4. Spacecraft laboratory
5. No verification	5. Remote sensing in-situ	5. Seismic sensors
	6. Remote sensing national technical means	6. Control posts
	7. Complaints consultation	7. Remote-sensing posts
	8. Collateral analysis	8. Peace-keeping observer missions
		9. Literature survey
		10. International information exchange

SOURCE: Report of the Secretary-General, *Reduction of Military Budgets* (New York: U.N. Department for Disarmament Affairs, 1983), pp. 96.

Table 2

Confidence-Building Measures

Illustrative Triptych

Detection of War Preparations	Clarification of Activities	Constraints on Preparedness
1. Observers	1. Advance notification and forecasts of maneuvers and other movements	1. Restricted deployment zones
2. On-call inspection		2. Activity constraints by size, location, duration and/or frequency
3. Non-concealment undertakings	2. Information exchange on activities and posture	
4. National Technical Means (NTM) noninterference	3. Direct communication links	
5. Ban on coded radio traffic		

SOURCE: Derived with modification from Jonathan Alford, "The Usefulness and the Limitations of CBMs," *New Directions in Disarmament*, William Epstein and Bernard T. Feld, eds. (New York: Praeger, 1981), p. 136.

PART VI

THE FUTURE OF ARMS CONTROL: A PANEL DISCUSSION

The Future of Arms Control:
A Panel Discussion

John Norton Moore: To pose just some of the issues, if we are to address the future of arms control we must discuss the complete range of negotiations from SALT and START to INF and the Mutual and Balanced Force Reduction (MBFR) talks. We should consider the United Nations' Committee on Disarmament process and the negotiations held under the auspices of the Committee for Disarmament in Europe (CDE). Also, Vice President Bush's proposal to ban chemical weapons, by prohibiting their production, stockpiling and use in a manner similar to the 1972 Biological Weapons Convention, merits our attention.

If we turn to the START negotiations and the central strategic front, there are a whole range of crucial and complex issues that confront us. Initial questions concerning the appropriate configuration and mix of the offensive strategic forces must be resolved. Should we, for example, embrace the "build-down" proposals as well as move to small, mobile single warhead ICBMs? The implications of moving beyond a triad to "quadrad" by employing a variety of long-range cruise missiles constitutes another problem area.

There is also the important question of the appropriate balance between strategic offensive systems and defensive forces. If the Soviet Union is conducting a major program on ballistic missile defense, can the United States and the West afford not to engage in a similar program? Should that program go beyond the laboratory research stage at any point? If so, what should be the configuration of the defensive strategic forces, and what will be the future of the 1972 Anti-Ballistic Missile Treaty? Should the ABM Treaty be renegotiated? Or should the United States exercise its right under Article XV to withdraw from the Treaty if it determines that its

149

"supreme interests" have been jeopardized? If the ABM Treaty is to be renegotiated, what kinds of changes will be necessary and what will be the most appropriate forum for undertaking the new negotiations?

In addition, negotiations such as START raise important questions about the verification of arms control agreements. Which of the parameters that are important in the arms control process are verifiable? Put another way, when keeping verification in mind, what kinds of things should we include and attempt to control in a strategic arms agreement?

In the Intermediate-range Nuclear Force talks we have a range of issues and questions similar to those encountered in the START process. We might also raise the issue, which has not yet been discussed, of the interrelationship between the long-range INF missiles, such as the SS-20 and Pershing II, and the shorter-range systems, such as the SS-21, SS-22 and SS-23, which the Soviets have been deploying on such a massive scale.

If we shift to some broader theoretical questions on arms control, we must consider how we can first achieve strategic stability. How do we, through discussion on both force structure and arms control, encourage a strategic environment that is more stable for both superpowers? And how do we achieve that goal when both sides have such different strategic force structures and such seemingly divergent views on arms control?

We should also focus on other kinds of theoretical issues such as identifying and blocking possible pathways to nuclear conflict. We must determine what are the most likely scenarios that would lead to nuclear war between the United States and the USSR, and then derive measures to prevent such a chain of events. Can we, for example, envisage a variety of new confidence-building measures which could be used to block a particular kind of pathway such as the accidental launch?

Another general problem area concerns the implications of Soviet noncompliance with arms control provisions. How should the West deal with this critical issue? What are the implications of Soviet noncompliance for arms control and strategic stability in general, and how do we more effectively seek Soviet compliance in the future?

Finally, I would like to pose a question that I think is quite important politically for the long-term outlook for arms control in this country and the West. To what extent do we have a problem, or an obligation, to bring into line expectations of realistic possibilities for arms control and disarmament with public expectations as to what is sought, and should be sought, through the arms control process? This problem is, of course, a double-edged weapon. On the one hand, the public could disapprove of arms control and seek to terminate a particular arms control effort. On the other hand, the public could believe that arms control holds greater promise than it can actually deliver in the real world. In the final analysis, it seems clear that conflicting beliefs and expectations between the government and the general public over the goals and utility of arms control could severely damage the arms control process over the long run, even in cases where negotiations have produced arms control agreements that are workable and beneficial.

With that rather brief introduction, I would like to call first Mr. Frank Gaffney, the Deputy Assistant Secretary of Defense for Strategic and Nuclear Policy.

Frank Gaffney: On the subject of the future of arms control I would like to discuss briefly three points. First, I would like to emphasize the important principle that arms control is not, and should not be regarded as, an end in itself. Second, I would like to apply that principle to the Reagan Administration's approach to arms control. Third, I would like to examine the difference between the Administration's approach to arms control and an alternative approach advocated by some proponents of arms control, and then suggest a conclusion of my own as to which course is preferable.

I think most experts, at least on the face of it, would agree that the principle that arms control is not an end in itself is a sound one. I think where the consensus may break down is when one asks what does that statement mean. I would like to highlight three points that I think are central to understanding this issue. First, the arms control process is not a process separate from that by which the United States national security as a whole is calculated. Arms control is an integral part of national security. Second, if arms control is to be productive and acceptable, it must be fully compatible with U.S. national security interests. Third, judgments about that compatibility must flow from a clear-eyed assessment of several factors.

One factor that must be considered is our experience to date with existing arms control agreements. This assessment should include reference to problems encountered during negotiations, difficulties with monitoring and verification, disagreements and ambiguities over language and interpretation, and, most important, the Soviet record of compliance and noncompliance with the agreements. Another factor that must be examined is how future arms control agreements will enhance U.S. national security. Arms control agreements should be crafted so that they are supportive of our national interest. This means that they must be verifiable. In addition, American negotiators should realistically anticipate what the Soviet Union's behavior will be under the agreement. Finally, allowance should be made for any so-called "soporific effect" the agreements might have on American military programs and defense decision-making. Arms control endeavors that lull the United States into a false sense of security or result in the cancellation of badly needed defense programs could jeopardize U.S. national security. In these cases national interest and arms control obviously would not be compatible.

I would submit that the Reagan Administration's approach to arms control has been fully consistent with both the underlying principle and the three-part analysis outlined above. This strategy should insure that arms control is an effective and integral element of our larger national security posture rather than an end in itself. Let me suggest several specific principles that I think underpin the Administration's approach to arms control and national security.

152

First, "cosmetic" arms control agreements, those that are unverifiable and prove not to be very meaningful militarily, are not adequate. Second, the Administration is prepared to propose and has proposed arms control measures, which if accepted by the Soviet Union, would result in significant enhancements to our security and that of the world at large. Third, in the meantime, we plan to acquire those military capabilities that we believe are needed to vouchsafe our deterrent and to protect world peace should it prove impossible to obtain the kind of arms control that we are seeking with the Soviet Union. Finally, we believe that the acquisition of such military capabilities can serve as an incentive to the Soviet Union to engage with us in real arms control negotiations. But if the Soviets should elect not to so do, we would still be protected and our deterrent would remain secure.

We believe that this four-part approach represents the best hope for the future of arms control. It would result in genuine arms control. Moreover, it would also make arms control an effective element in a resilient United States national security policy.

Ironically, there are others who oppose this approach even as they pay lip-service to the underlying principle that arms control is not an end in itself. They do so perhaps out of a misunderstanding of what our policy is, but also because they believe that there is some merit to pursuing arms control for its own sake. Examples of this sort of alternative approach include the desire for impromptu and quite possibly unproductive summit meetings between national leaders, the ratification of flawed treaties, and the tolerance of treaties even when we know, or strongly suspect, the Soviets are violating them. This other approach--arms control for the sake of arms control--also encourages negotiations toward agreements of dubious value such as an anti-satellite treaty or a comprehensive test ban. What is more, this view also influences Congress to undertake unilateral restraints in U.S. military programs, ostensibly driven by a belief that we need to do so in order to advance the cause of arms control. In my view, such initiatives represent or epitomize what I would call "bad" arms control.

Unfortunately, many people who have opposed this alternative approach have been undeservedly reviled as being impediments to arms control. I believe that one should not be ashamed about attempting to discriminate between good and bad arms control. Nor should one be ashamed to oppose bad arms control. I believe that if we do not oppose it, this alternative approach that I have described will result, at best, in a greater strategic imbalance and in further Soviet noncompliance with existing arms control agreements. At worst, it could jeopardize the very stability and global peace that we hope to preserve.

Let me say a further word about those who advocate this alternative approach. I believe they may well pose the greatest threat to real arms control. By advocating as they sometimes appear to do the "cover-up" of Soviet noncompliance with existing arms control agreements by insisting upon endless deliberations in the SCC or by delegating this avenue of inquiry to very quiet diplomacy, they debase the value of those accords and insure a continuation and, quite possibly, a worsening pattern of Soviet noncompliance. Furthermore, by incorrectly equating U.S. and Soviet behavior and by castigating the Administration's arms control efforts, I think such partisans undermine the prospects for serious negotiations in the future. An example of this problem is the aborted effort in March of 1977 by President Carter to obtain real arms reductions. This effort was effectively undercut by individuals in his own administration who argued that it was an unproductive course of action. I think that Congress in the many steps it has taken in the past month has perhaps done likewise with respect to ongoing efforts. Finally, by supporting this alternative approach I believe such partisans are fostering in the public mind, and to some extent in Congress as well, wholly unachievable and indeed undesirable expectations about what arms control can and should do.

Let me summarize. We stand at a critical crossroads in U.S. arms control policy. If we choose a sensible and realistic path, one which is advocated by the Reagan Administration, the future of real arms control as a component of effective national security is bright. However, if we choose the other approach, that of cosmetic arms control, tolerance of Soviet noncompliance, and, most importantly, inflation of unrealistic public expectations regarding the overall utility of arms control, I believe that neither the future of arms control nor the outlook for American security is bright.

John Norton Moore: Our next speaker is John B. Rhinelander, who was the Legal Adviser to the U.S. SALT I Delegation.

John Rhinelander: My overall sense is that the process of arms control as we have known it over the last 15 to 25 years is breaking down. We can talk about "real" and "good" arms control, but these are just normative terms. What is real to one person may be impossible or unachievable to another. One can describe the arms control process in different ways and attach all sorts of various labels, but what most concerns me is the outlook for the process itself.

On every issue that comes up in the international context with the Soviets, you really only have to deal with two fundamental questions. One is whether the U.S. wishes to limit or restrict the Soviet Union from undertaking a particular military activity. If the answer is yes, then this means the U.S. would also have to restrict its own activities that are similar. The other question, which is really only the converse of the first one, is whether the U.S. ought to be free to do something. If the U.S. decides not to restrain itself, then of course the Soviets would be free to do the same thing.

The problem with this analytical approach is that the two superpowers often do not have the same forces, programs or objectives at the same time. The result is that it can be extremely difficult to obtain an arms control agreement, much less one that is "real" or in the best interests of the United States. For example, during the 1960s we had more ICBM launchers than did the Soviet Union. When SALT I began we proposed a freeze on ICBM launchers. The Soviets, of course, did not agree to this proposal. They effectively stonewalled us, and by the time we reached the Interim Agreement in 1972 their numbers of launchers had exceeded ours. What is realistic and what is possible are really only in the eyes of the beholder.

Let me go to the compliance questions because they are a major part of the problem that we face today in arms control. We are focusing on, and should focus on, Soviet noncompliance. I think that what the Soviets are doing with the large Krasnoyarsk radar in Siberia is a serious problem. It is not a central issue militarily, but it is a clear violation of the 1972 ABM Treaty. On the other hand, some of the activities the United States is doing in terms of the SDI program, while not as serious as the Russian radar at the moment, will in effect constitute a frontal assault on the ABM Treaty. This is also a serious problem. But when compliance issues are discussed generally in forums such as this, they always focus on Soviet noncompliance. We must remember that compliance is a two-way street.

Michael Krepon was correct yesterday when he said the ABM Treaty was breaking down and that both sides were hedging. It is going to be up to both governments to decide in the end whether it is in their interests, individually and jointly, to remain part of a bilateral arms control process or whether they should instead go their own separate ways. To borrow a phrase, I think the jury is still out on this issue.

The arms control process which had developed up through 1972 began to run into obstacles for several reasons. The impact of the Vietnam War on our country, the divisiveness of Watergate, and our suspicions regarding the Soviets all played a role. But other factors were involved as well. One of the problems has to do with the nature of any legal agreement. Agreements often become an exercise as to what you can do which is not prohibited. They become invitations to design around their prohibitions. I think that this is one of the problems that we are seeing right now with the ABM Treaty. This problem is one of the greatest challenges in the field of arms control.

In 1972 we established the Standing Consultative Commission as part of the ABM treaty. It was one of the most significant steps we took, but I think it has only been half utilized so far. The SCC has focused mainly on compliance issues. However, there is another problem area that must be dealt with as well in either the SCC or in another forum. We must deal with ongoing questions of technological change as they come up. For example, are we going to limit a new kind of activity at the outset? Are we going to set precise limits on it? Or are we not?

I think most of the compliance issues that we hear about these days in the field of the SALT agreements are ones where it is not a question of what the facts are, but rather it is a question of what is the limit of the legal prohibitions. It is a question of legal drafting and treaty interpretation. The question of what does "develop" mean? What does "capability" mean? These are some of the questions on the ABM side.

With regard to SALT II one of the questions the Reagan administration has asked, and it is a legitimate question, is whether the Soviets are violating what was called the "one new type" rule for new ICBMs. Now I was not part of the SALT II negotiation, but I know a fair amount about it and one of the things the U.S. did at SALT II was to fudge on a tight definition because we did not know which way we wanted to go with the MX, our next ICBM design. The Soviets had proposed some tighter definitions at SALT II which we had rejected. Now the tables have been turned on us. The definition is not as tight as it could have been, and clearly as it should have been, if we were going to have a nice, clean standard against which to judge this compliance issue.

When you go through a lot of these agreements and look at the ambiguities, sometimes you will find that they were purposefully left that way because both sides were hedging and did not want to restrict their future flexibility. On other occasions one or the other wanted to eliminate the ambiguity and the other side simply said no. Again, during SALT I we tried to close off what was clearly going to be the Soviets next ICBM. They would not agree to this. I think we perhaps misled ourselves. We may have misled Congress in terms of what that agreement allowed. As a result, there was a great furor when the Soviets produced the SS-18, which was larger than any ICBM we had seen before. This problem was a result of the failure to tighten up the agreement.

Now from time to time there have been statements in the public saying we ought to keep these things nice and simple. It is said that the public and the members of Congress can not really understand complex arms control agreements. But the problem is that we are dealing with complex technologies. If the problem you are dealing with is complex, I think your response to it has to be complex. There are legitimate questions now being asked in the Pentagon. What can we do that will be consistent with the treaties? What can't we do? And if we are going to have rules which we are going to abide by, and which we expect the Soviets to abide by, those agreements are going to have to be quite specific. I think that this is the heart of the compliance problem, or at least most of the compliance questions.

The real challenge that we are going to face in many of these areas is this: can we respond diplomatically in the arms control field to the pace of technological change? The jury is still out. The SALT process has definitely been behind the curve over these years. We clearly had a chance in the 1969-1972 period to limit what has now become the most difficult problem in this whole field, the so-called MIRV (multiple independently targetable reentry vehicle) problem. We made a proposal to the Soviets which we knew was nonnegotiable. They made one back to us which they knew was non-negotiable. Thus, we agreed not to negotiate. That is what brought us to the problem where we are now. And now there is a lot of thought about going back to single warhead missiles. The world would be a lot simpler.

But it is very tough to turn the clock back. One of the problems in this field is timing. The window of opportunity is open for only a relatively short period of time, and if you do not move at that point your problem is going to be much more difficult later. The MIRV problem was one example, and cruise missiles are another one which we have right now. It is going to be extremely difficult to get a handle on cruise missiles given the fact that both the U.S. and the Soviet Union have been deploying them in rather sophisticated ways. When you lose the opportunity to act on a particular problem, the way in which you can deal with it in the future is made much more difficult, if not impossible.

John Norton Moore: Our next panelist is Ambassador Raymond Garthoff. Ray has a long and distinguished background in the SALT negotiations.

Ray Garthoff: I would like to stress again at the outset a point that I made very briefly yesterday. The interrelation and interaction between our overall political situation and arms control is extremely important. Arms control, we are all agreed, is not an end in itself and should not be thought of as such. But the main reason we need arms control is precisely because we face a formidable adversary. If we did not have this adversarial relationship with the Soviet Union, arms control would be much less important and much less necessary. So, the arms control process is not something that should be put off or held to what is minimally convenient until there is some improvement in political relations. On the contrary, it is because of the threat of the arms race, the possibilities of nuclear war, and the other dangers of an uncontrolled arms competition that we need to approach seriously arms control and do what can be done to improve our security interests.

Clearly, we all agree that we should pursue good arms control and eschew bad arms control. I, for example, could not agree more with Mr. Gaffney on that principle. However, I could not disagree with him more on the examples that he mentioned. I think that anti-satellite arms control, a comprehensive nuclear test ban, and building on the SALT process are precisely those areas where we can and should be doing more.

I would like to deal briefly with just two general areas. First, there is the whole question of the different perspectives of the two sides and their differing perceptions. This is a difficult problem psychologically, and sometimes politically as well. It is hard to make the distinction which exists between empathy, trying to put yourself in the position of the other side, and sympathy. One can and should try to understand how the opponent, or anyone else, looks at the situation and views his interests without necessarily accepting his point of view. This is something that is very difficult for analysts to do. It is even more difficult for policymakers to accomplish, particularly in the Soviet Union and the United States. It is not easy sometimes to determine the real perceptions of the other side. One does have to do a lot of filtering out from propaganda and other intended purposes of statements and actions. The military balance in Europe and between the superpowers are questions which seemingly deal with objective factors such as numbers and characteristics of weapons. In fact, these issues are highly subjective. They all depend on what factors you put in to the equation. The conclusions you get are going to depend on the assumptions, premises or parameters you used when making the analysis.

The issue of confidence in security-building measures is another very important area. The Reagan administration seems to have recognized the value of this subject, and to have made some efforts to discuss it quietly with the Soviets. This is a positive step, but I have only modest expectations for both the bilateral exchange and the multilateral exchanges at the CDE and the MBFR. However, I certainly think we are on the right track. We should continue to pursue confidence-building measures and do what we can to the fullest possible extent.

When negotiations on confidence-building measures extend over into more heavily political content, they become more difficult but also potentially more promising. These kind of negotiations will depend even more on a minimum degree of acceptance of

160

serious interests on the part of the adversary. For example, the question that our chairman posed of looking into the question of normative questions on the nonuse of force is a very important one. But it cuts a couple of ways. The Monroe Doctrine, and perhaps the Carter Doctrine, could also be problematical for the United States. If one begins to look at what rules of the game you want to apply to the adversary, you have to take account of how they would affect our own freedom of action and our own patterns of action.

Stability is the second major area I wanted to mention briefly. Strategic stability was noted as being sufficiently important to be the main theme for this conference. I just want to point out there are four aspects to the notion of stability. One is stability as an aim or goal. This is important, but hardly enough alone. Incidentally, the United States and the Soviet Union in confidential talks during the pre-SALT discussions in 1968 agreed formally on seeking the goal of stability in what was to become the SALT enterprise. This goal was restated many times in SALT. The problem is not one of agreeing to stability as an aim. The problem is one of deciding how to apply and use this concept in concrete terms.

Another aspect of stability is as a decision-making criterion. Once again, this is a very important concept, but it is also something that we tend to apply as convenient. I do not think there is any way in which a rigorous application of considerations of stability would have allowed a decision to proceed with the deployment of the Pershing II missile, for example.

The third aspect of stability is as a rationale. This is the most questionable aspect of all. We talked a great deal in SALT I, for example, about stability with respect to various proposals that we made. So did the Soviets. In fact, during the SALT process, to take just one example, we completely flip-flopped four times on the question of whether a mobile land-based ICBM was stabilizing or destabilizing. The result was that at the time the SALT I agreements were signed we made a stern, unilateral statement that any

161

deployment of a land-based ICBM would be inconsistent with the purposes of the agreement. By the time the SALT II negotiations were underway, the Soviets were trying to get us to limit mobile land-based ICBMs. The most we would grudgingly concede was to put a stipulation in a protocol agreement not to deploy mobile ICBMs for three years. We made it very clear, though, that we agreed to this provision because we were not ready to deploy mobile ICBMS during those three years anyway. We also said that we were going to continue to develop mobile ICBMs and deploy them when we could. There is nothing wrong with this approach. The Soviets, incidentally, also reversed field a number of times in their use of stability as a rationale for particular positions that they advanced. I will say one difference is that we got ahead of them, in a sense, by withdrawing positions on these two occasions after they had already been accepted by the Soviets. This is not a good procedure in general.

Finally, there is stability as a result. This is, of course, what ultimately counts although some of the other aspects of stability are important too. One example has already been mentioned in this regard. We succeeded in our efforts to keep MIRVs alive in SALT I. We now generally accept that the result was destabilizing. Similarly, deep reductions are desirable for a number of reasons, but I do not think they are necessarily the main element in seeking stability. Furthermore, under some circumstances they could even be destabilizing. In this regard, the Reagan Administration has put such a heavy stress on reductions in START mainly, I believe, in order to disarm the disarmers by advocating a position which goes further than either a nuclear freeze or the SALT agreements. The net result was that any kind of arms control agreement remained virtually unattainable. Also, deep reductions at a certain point also increase sensitivity to monitoring and verification problems and amplify the threat posed by third country nuclear forces.

John Norton Moore: Our last speaker is Robert W.

Dean, who is the Deputy Assistant Secretary for Arms Control at the Department of State.

Robert Dean: The issue before this nation is how to achieve and maintain a more stable nuclear balance. The title of this panel should be "The Future of the Nuclear Balance." That said, it is clear to the Administration that the security of the United States and the Soviet Union can be improved by achieving lower levels of nuclear forces. This axiom will continue to guide our policies.

With regard to the future of arms control, let me offer five factors which I think will have a controlling effect over the next five years on the course of arms control. The first is Soviet behavior in the international arena. It is the case that an assertive Soviet foreign policy is not conducive to arms control. We were chastened after the experience of the 1970s when a host of East-West agreements which sought to reorder the nuclear relationship between the West and the Soviet Union were achieved at the same time the Soviets undertook a very aggressive modernization program with respect to their conventional and strategic forces. This is not a benign phenomenon. It is something that we and our European allies have to take seriously. We have to take the Soviet military buildup as a starting point in our approach to the Soviet Union, and as a factor in our own arms control policies. It is a political fact of life that the arms control process is a product of the overall U.S.-Soviet relationship.

Second, the consolidation of the Soviet leadership itself is another important factor. We have no reason to suspect that the Chernenko leadership, the third Soviet leadership in three years, lacks internal discipline. For example, they have undertaken an initiative in space arms control during this hiatus of negotiations and have even urged us to come back to the table. They sat down with us in January at the Conference on Disarmament in Europe in Stockholm. Clearly, they can act dispassionately when they can identify areas of negotiation that are in their own interests. They have not taken their ball and walked

163

away from the field. And they will come back to the negotiation table. But, with respect to the leadership itself, the bureaucratic discipline of the Brezhnev era is clearly missing. Inevitably, this complicates Soviet planning as well as their conduct of negotiations and ability to reach agreements with the United States.

A third factor with respect to the future of arms control is the continuity and progress we are able to make in our own strategic modernization programs. One strong incentive that the Soviet Union has always had to engage the United States in arms control, and this was true in the late 1960s and early 1970s as well as it is today, is to stop or slow our strategic programs. Their engagement in the arms process, in part, is due to the fact that this gives them political control over our strategic programs. It is, therefore, essential that we not do the Soviets' job for them. We must continue with our own strategic modernization programs in order to provide the Soviets with an incentive to regulate these forces in both of our mutual interests.

Fourth, the smaller size and the increased mobility of newer nuclear systems will be a determining factor over the next five years. These systems will present difficulties for verification and monitoring, and will necessitate a more open and creative approach to verification. The old verification methods, that is, the simple reliance on national technical means, simply will not do. This will be as true for a Democratic administration as it will be for a Republican administration.

Finally, we face the problem of the resolution of compliance and verification questions that are outstanding. The Soviets have clearly demonstrated that they are willing to push existing agreements to their limits and beyond. This has clearly jeopardized the arms control process. We cannot simply sweep these activities under the rug, and I submit to you that a Democratic administration will have to cope with this problem equally as much as we.

I would like to make a few brief comments on points that have already been raised. I am not sure I am interpreting what John Rhinelander said correctly, but in my view, with all deference to his very fine comments, the solution to arms control is not necessarily fine-tuning or adding precision to the language of treaties. As a means of channeling or controlling technologies any legal document will always have gray areas. It will always be subject to interpretation. Most importantly, I think it is a mistake to suggest that tighter definitions in the ABM Treaty would have prevented the Soviets from taking a decision at the highest level to build the illegal radar at Krasnoyarsk. The treaty language is crystal-clear on this issue. Greater precision would not have helped.

The Soviet leadership knows what it is doing with respect to this radar. They have chosen to go ahead at Krasnoyarsk and take their chances with the ABM Treaty. Furthermore, it is inconceivable that this decision was not made at the Politburo level.

A point that Ray Garthoff made, or perhaps only alluded to, has to do with the levels of rhetoric on both sides. I feel that it is a mistake to believe the rhetoric that has been used on both sides over the past few years has any effect whatsoever on the course of negotiations. If you pick up *Pravda* on any day at random and turn to the editorial page, you will be treated to a vilification of President Reagan and the United States. However, we have rarely reciprocated in an equivalent manner. Hyperbole and purple prose are not the stuff of international politics. Wounded pride is not a factor and has not been a determining factor over the course of the last three years.

Finally, I would like to respond to a point made earlier suggesting that Congress is trying to restrain the arms race. I would suggest that congressional activity over the past three weeks has demonstrated that the American people understand the necessity of a creditable United States defense posture and the need for a cautious, deliberate approach in formulating American policy toward the Soviet Union. During the storms of debate over ASATs, sea-launched cruise missiles (SLCMs), and the SALT interim restraints issue, the Senate authorized virtually the entire funding request of the President for defense programs. There is a mood of unease in the country about nuclear issues, but as one who has spent a great deal of time over the past three years discussing these issues with groups all over the country I would argue that the political center of gravity and the wisdom of the American people is very much reflected in the Administration's approach to arms control.

John Norton Moore: I would like to give our panelists a very brief opportunity to make one or two more comments, or to ask a question to any other panelist or the panel as a whole. I would like to start with Mr. Frank Gaffney.

Frank Gaffney: I think that this has been a useful exchange. It has really clearly delineated the spectrum of approaches to the subject. I am satisfied that I have not incorrectly characterized what I think are bad arms control ideas. While we may disagree over the best terms for defining "bad arms control," I think that you can appreciate that there was a rather dramatic difference in the willingness of some of the panelists to engage in the kinds of elements of what I would call a bad arms approach. For example, they have shown a willingness to enter into negotiations on agreements which I think we can realistically describe as being inimical to the maintenance of a credible nuclear deterrent. In this regard, I would offer to you as an example the idea of a comprehensive ban on nuclear testing.

At this point, I would like to raise a concern I have about the extent to which in selling the previous arms control agreements to the Congress, "selling" being a crass word but nonetheless I think an accurate one, the Congress was misled about what these treaties were intended to do and what they could actually accomplish. What I would like to ask John Rhinelander is this: who was selling these treaties if not the people who negotiated them? It seems to me that the administrations who negotiated these treaties understood precisely the limitations that were consciously built into them, and yet they were prepared to go to the Congress and say that the

166

treaties were going to provide for more restraints than they actually did.

John Rhinelander: Let me take a shot at Frank Gaffney's question, and Ray Garthoff may want to add something. I think in terms of SALT I Henry Kissinger was doing the major selling. Kissinger is a fascinating and interesting man. I do not think technical details are of enormous interest to him at times.

One of the great problems with the SALT I Interim Agreement, frankly, is what happened in Moscow with the Summit. As you recall, the U.S. SALT I delegation was left back in Helsinki. We had several alternatives for whatever policy decision the President wished to make. But Kissinger negotiated virtually alone in Moscow, and in some cases he reached agreement with the Soviets on terms that were less favorable than we had achieved back at Helsinki. Moreover, some of the treaty language adopted by Kissinger was totally opaque. And on that basis, then, the administration went forward and presented to the Congress a treaty which was really not clear.

There are still some questions from SALT I which I do not yet know the answers. For example, the old Soviet SLBM submarines, the Golf boats and the Hotel boats, remain a puzzle. It still has not been clarified as to what Kissinger meant when he negotiated Article III of the Interim Agreement in Moscow. He went there without an American interpreter, and this part of the negotiation was really behind the back of Gerard Smith, the chairman of the U.S. SALT I delegation. It was a hell of a way to run a negotiation. I think that this kind of behavior has not been done since, and I hope it is never done again. While these drafting mistakes did not concern central issues, they clearly upset in this country attempts to agree to and comply with the terms of the agreement. And I think that this lesson is something which is always going to be important for us to remember.

Let me go to one other point that Mr. Gaffney made in terms of the comparative seriousness of violations. The basic point I want to make is that no matter what our intentions are, if we are both interpreting the language and meaning of a legal agreement as well as interpreting the facts pertaining to the agreement, there will always be opportunities for others to disagree reasonably with us. In our domestic setting we have courts, and the best of people may think their position is very good, but they find when they go before a federal judge that he disagrees with them. What we are basically doing now is judging the Soviets by our own standards. What I would like to suggest is that while the Soviets may not agree with us, even a third party, if one were to exist, might not necessarily agree with us on some issues.

There are a range of things which the U.S. has done that legitimately raise questions under these agreements. The environmental shelters, which we placed over our ICBM silos while we worked on them, is a classic case in point. Our actions in this regard were stupid. It did not hurt the Soviets one bit--they still knew exactly what we were doing because they could read about these activities in the *Congressional Record*. Nonetheless, we clearly did something which was in violation of SALT I. The Air Force was ordered to take the shelters down, but they would not remove them. This is the kind of action which if it were done by the Soviets would send us "up the trees." If they had done it, we would not necessarily have known what they were doing and it would have been a serious problem. In our case, because they knew what we were doing, it did not raise a problem in terms of whether we were breaking out of the agreement or doing something which was unlawful. But it clearly was in violation of the agreement, and we put in the provision against concealment for good reasons. The satellites could not see what was going on underneath the shelters.

In terms of other areas of possible U.S. arms control violations, I think that what we are doing in the SDI program is clearly going to result in violation of the ABM Treaty. I have talked to some very high-level people on a confidential basis at the Pentagon, and they admit that what we are doing, or what we have announced we plan to do, will be in violation of the Treaty in 1986. However, they claim there will not be a violation because we intend to amend the agreement by then. This is a phony argument. It assumes that the Soviets will agree to amend the Treaty so that what we intend to do will be by then legal. This is clearly a charade. In the final analysis, both sides are going to have to live by the agreements, and this means live by limitations which are going to effect adversely their programs. If the United States and the Soviet Union do not abide by their agreements, the arms control process is going to fail eventually.

Ray Garthoff: I would like to pick up the point that Bob Dean mentioned about the Soviet decision to deploy the Krasnoyarsk radar in Siberia. He said that it was inconceivable this was not a decision based in the Politburo. We do not know anything about the precise decision mechanism involved, but I think it is extremely unlikely that it was a deliberate decision made at the Politburo level. Let me suggest the way it probably occurred.

Probably at a very high level in the Soviet General Staff someone proposed that an additional radar be built into the large early warning radar system that had been pushed around the periphery of the country in accordance with the ABM Treaty. It made a lot of sense to put the Krasnoyarsk radar deep in Siberia in order to cover the flight cone of missiles launched from American Trident submarines in the North Pacific. The military personnel making this decision probably knew the ABM Treaty provides that early warning radars are supposed to be located on the periphery and oriented outward. But perhaps someone pointed out that the ABM Treaty also said that you can build a space track radar of the same general type as an early warning radar any place inside the USSR. So they decided to give the radar some of the characteristics of a space tracking radar. They really do not need it there for space tracking, but they could at least use that as an ostensible legal justification for its existence while it served its early warning purpose.

I am not suggesting that is a good way to approach this decision at all. I think it was not, but I would suspect that a discussion along that line took place at a level high within the military but below the political level. It was probably then cursorily approved as a budget line item along with a lot of other things in the defense council and, conceivably, in the Politburo. I do not think anyone proposed to any Soviet political leader, "Let's violate the ABM Treaty by putting this early warning radar inland where it's not supposed to be."

Now, what about the American deployment of the PAVE PAWS early warning radars? We have two of those installed, and two more are going to be located in Georgia and Texas. They are very close to the border of the United States. Thus, there is no question that they are deployed along the periphery. This fulfills one of the two considerations required by the ABM Treaty. The other condition imposed by the Treaty is that the radars be oriented outward. Now the Soviet radars have solid, flat faces facing outward so that they do not present a compliance problem. It will be recalled that the problem with the Krasnayarsk radar was that it was put inland.

Our early warning radars, however, do not have a single, flat face facing outward. So even though they are on the periphery, they each have a 240 degree angle which can cover a great deal of the continental United States. Therefore, they inherently provide a potential for an ABM battle management radar system. There is no question that the United States is planning to use them for that purpose, but a real question can be raised, and has been, as to whether these radars are fully in compliance with the ABM Treaty. Significantly, the decision about these radars was not made by President Reagan. No one went to him and asked, "Shall we build this radar in this way even though we know it covers a good bit of the United States and therefore can be said to be in violation of the ABM Treaty?"

This problem is part of the question that was raised yesterday about technical violations and whether they are necessarily cheating, or whether a violation may be deliberate at one level and yet in another sense not necessarily constitute a national political decision to violate a treaty. Of course, there may be cases in which some national political decisions have been made to violate treaties. Take one other example. Recently, the United States fired an experimental anti-ballistic missile which successfully intercepted an ICBM warhead at a very high altitude. This test was part of the Homing Overlay Experiment (HOE). It was a very considerable technical achievement. It is permitted by the ABM Treaty to test ABM systems as long as only fixed, land-based interceptors are used. However, the missile we used for this interception experiment was an old Minuteman I ICBM. The ABM Treaty, Article IV, paragraph (a), prohibits the use of any missile for testing in an ABM mode, which this admittedly was, except an ABM interceptor. Significantly, the Minuteman is not an ABM interceptor. As a result, this test was at least a probable violation of the ABM Treaty. The Soviets have hedged on this test, but how many Americans have realized that? We are not applying the same standard. The best standard to apply is, as John Rhinelander mentioned previously, to ask what would we think if the Soviets undertook a similar activity. If we applied that standard to each of our own actions, we would find that it is not always as simple as it seems to determine whether the other side is in compliance.

We should take these ABM compliance matters to the Standing Consultative Commission (SCC). We had questions about what testing in ABM mode meant in the 1970s and some of the arguments that we used then have been overtaken by a supplementary agreement reached in the SCC which is now applied by both sides. Consequently, we are now proceeding with some programs which I think are probably going to be in compliance with that agreement, but which are not in keeping with what the United States was arguing as the proper interpretation of that point eight years ago. So these issues do not pose absolute questions. There are problems that have to be worked out; and they can best be resolved if the question is posed and discussed in a quiet and neutral forum. The Soviets did not go public during that whole four-year period when they were trying to get us to remove those environmental shelters. They did that all privately, even though it took several years to get the shelters off after we told the Soviets that they would be removed. On the other hand, when the President issues a public bill of indictment about a possible Soviet violation, it is very difficult to then go back and work out any kind of understanding which we can apply to both countries. We do not want them to be able to undertake actions under the agreement that we are unable to do, but we also should not want to be able to do things ourselves that are not in keeping with the standard we want to apply to the Soviets.

Herbert Scoville: I would like to ask Frank Gaffney why he stated that an ASAT agreement would be of dubious value, and why that is his opinion. Furthermore, is this the opinion of the U.S. government at the moment? It seems to me very clear that it is to our advantage to stop an arms race in space. After all, we rely so much more on space for our military superiority and military activities than does the Soviet Union.

Also, I would like to ask Bob Dean to explain what alternatives he has in mind when he made the statement that national technical means will not suffice for verification in the future. Now, if he is referring to the fact that we must have on-site inspections for all kinds of verification procedures, I wonder if he has looked at the practical measures for on-site inspections for which there is some hope of achieving and which we would accept in this country. How much would such measures really add to our confidence in verification? For example, I found rather interesting the on-site inspection provisions that were in the draft U.S. chemical weapons treaty which was strongly endorsed in one of the sessions yesterday. The provisions were carefully worded so that the United States would not have to accept inspection of Monsanto, DuPont and other private chemical centers. It was thought that this would be unacceptable to the public in the United States. On the other hand, since everything in the Soviet Union is under national control, the treaty would have given the United States the right to inspect everything in the Soviet Union. That kind of an on-site inspection provision is certainly not negotiable from the standpoint of the Soviet Union. Thus, this alternative at any rate hardly constitutes a realistic substitute for our standard national technical means of verification.

John Norton Moore: Next I would like to call on Bob Dean, who can answer Pete Scoville's question in passing. Then I am going to give Frank Gaffney and John Rhinelander a chance to respond briefly to the questions posed by Dr. Scoville.

Robert Dean: National technical means will have to be augmented to achieve verification on a case-by-case basis. It is difficult to speak generally about the problem. One can imagine a continuum in terms of augmentation that runs from a greater exchange of information which will help us decipher the characteristics of Soviet systems about which we are now in the dark to various on-site inspection measures where they are appropriate and/or required. There may be more than one way to resolve the problem with respect to various verification and monitoring regimes. I simply posed the question in my remarks because I think it is a determining factor. We have hardly been asleep on this. We have devoted a great deal of effort over the past three or four years to looking at issues such as SLCM and GLCM verification. A lot can be done with on-site sensors. Also, a lot can be done through the exchange of information. This problem does not necessarily mean that teams of Americans will be roving the Soviet Union looking for hidden cruise missiles, which is often the way that it is painted in the press or the character that some impose upon the whole idea of intrusive on-site inspection. Intrusive on-site inspection is possible and workable.

Frank Gaffney: I think that the central point with respect to the statements made by John Rhinelander about environmental shelters and Ray Garthoff about PAVE PAWS and the homing overlay experiment is that the disparity that exists between Soviet understandings of our capabilities and intentions, and our knowledge of Soviet capabilities and intentions is serious. Soviet access to the *Congressional Record*, hearings before Congress, and the Secretary of Defense's posture statement, especially when coupled with their own existing legal and illegal on-site inspection measures in the U.S., make the information imbalance very significant. This has to affect the extent to which we should equate their concerns about verification and violations with our own concerns about their questionable activities.

Finally, I would like to address the ASAT issue. This is one of those cases where we do not have a clear understanding of what the Soviets are doing. Moreover, the notion that there is an upcoming space arms race is a fraud. And I say that as starkly as I do because this misapprehension has been predicated upon enormous amounts of debate in Congress and elsewhere. It is simply the case that the Soviet Union is in space today, and they are there to stay. They are making use of it for direct military purposes, and our ability to constrain their activities credibly and in a verifiable fashion through an arms control agreement is at best limited. This is what compels me to say that such an agreement would be of dubious value.

John Rhinelander: Let me just respond to Bob Dean, who made a comment to the effect that tightening up treaty language will not always solve arms control problems. I agree with that. He also said that there will always be gray areas, and I agree with that. And he concluded by saying a tighter definition would not have helped with respect to the Krasnayarsk radar in Siberia. I do not agree with that statement because this was a question we looked at very carefully during SALT. The only way to deal with, or to avoid, the kind of compliance questions which we have now with regard to these large space tracking radars was to have a rule which said that neither country could build any without the consent of the other. This rule was totally unacceptable to the U.S. government during the negotiation of the SALT agreements for good reason. We knew there would be a problem in this area because these space track radars were totally unconstrained by the ABM Treaty. Also, the problem is not one of technology *per se*. The problem with radar technology is that it can be used for many purposes. The question is, what is the technology going to be used for? This was an issue that was bound to raise questions. There was a way to prevent ambiguity and compliance questions, but that answer was simply unacceptable to us as a government and probably would have been unacceptable to the Soviets at the same time. And therefore we now have this ABM radar question.

I would like to go back to the compliance question. It is true that the environmental shelters were not a serious question. But the Talon Gold project, which is part of the Strategic Defense Initiative, is a serious problem. Casper Weinberger's posture statement in 1984 announced what the Talon Gold program was going to do, and gave its schedule. As it was described, it will be on a collision course with the ABM Treaty by 1986 or 1987. I think that this project is just as serious a problem as the Soviet Krasnayarsk radar which, incidentally, will not be operational until around 1989.